AMERICAN PIT BULL TERRIER

FROM THE EDITORS OF **DOGFANCY** MAGAZINE

SMART OWNER'S GUIDE®

CONTENTS

American Pit Bull Terrier, a Smart Owner's Guide®
part of the Kennel Club Books® Interactive Series®
ISBN: 978-1-593787-59-2. ©2009

Kennel Club Books Inc., 40 Broad St., Freehold, NJ 07728. Printed in China.
All rights reserved. No part of this book may be reproduced in any form,
by Photostat, scanner, microfilm, xerograph, or any other means, or incorporated
into any information retrieval system, electronic or mechanical,
without the written permission of the copyright owner.

photographers include Isabelle Francias/BowTie Inc., Tara Darling,
Gina Cioli and Pamela Hunnicutt. Contributing writer: F. Favorito

For CIP information, see page 176.
14 13 12 11   3 4 5 6 7 8 9 10

K9 EXPERT

If you have purchased an American Pit Bull Terrier from a responsible breeder or adopted one from a shelter — or are planning to do so — congratulations! You are among the true dog lovers who think for yourselves and don't believe the old wives' tales that circulate in the world of dogs and have tarnished many a fine breed's reputation.

Surely no breed has been demonized to the extent that the pit bull has. At the same time that there are loving pit bulls doing pet visitation at seniors' facilities and children's hospitals, there are countless communities across the nation that have banned all manner of dogs that bear even the slightest resemblance to the pit bull. This knee-jerk response to a proud and noble all-American creation is a sad state of affairs. Thankfully, there are compassionate dog lovers with big hearts — much like yourselves — who have made the acceptance of pit bulls their personal crusade, their labor of love. We wish them luck in their endeavors.

Perhaps no breed of dog is a greater reflection of the care — or neglect — he receives at the hands of his owner than the pit bull. As well-informed dog lovers and trainers know, there is no inherently evil breed. Every dog starts his life as a blank slate. A positive home that has made a conscious choice to have an American Pit Bull Terrier join the family for all the right reasons can accomplish so much with this breed. No dog is more versatile or more loving to his people. The truth is that the pit bull makes a poor watch dog because the breed is friendly, even toward strangers. Aggression is uncharacteristic in this breed and has always been considered highly undesirable. The breed's love of children is especially well-known.

LOW MAINTENANCE

This is a spit-and-polish breed when it comes to grooming. Regular ear cleaning and nail cutting, along with an occasional

brushing, are all that's required. In the food department, the pit bull is known as an easy keeper. This is a generally healthy dog with a good appetite. In fact, the pit bull can be stoic in terms of enduring pain, so you need to be your dog's advocate, checking his eyes, ears, teeth and skin regularly to make sure all is well.

While grooming and feeding will be routine chores, where you must invest time is in socializing and training your pit bull. Most pit bulls will display some level of dog aggression. Couple that trait with his powerful physique and it is clear the pit bull requires an owner who will carefully socialize and obedience train the dog.

The earlier the socialization begins, the better. Puppy kindergarten classes are an excellent way to expose your dog to other breeds of varying temperaments. The public is less fearful of puppies than it is of adults. By having your dog walk calmly and happily by your side, eager to greet strangers, your neighbors will see a pit bull well integrated into the community.

Take advantage of any and all opportunities to demonstrate your dog's biddable temperament in parks, schools and community events. Show people that you have a sweet, affectionate dog who just happens to be a pit bull. The effort you make will send an important message to society — dog owners and non-dog owners alike.

Your pit bull needs your affection and approval, but these alone won't create a well-adjusted dog. Set limits and boundaries for your dog, be consistent in your training and acknowledge your responsibility as a pit bull owner. Accepting these

With this Smart Owner's Guide®, you are well on your way to getting your APBT diploma.
But your American Pit Bull Terrier education doesn't end here. You're invited to join **Club APBT®** (**DogChannel.com/Club-APBT**), a FREE online site with lots of fun and instructive online features like:
◆ **forums, blogs** and **profiles** to connect with other pit bull owners
◆ **downloadable charts** and **checklists** to help you be a smart and loving American Pit Bull Terrier owner
◆ access to APBT-specific **e-cards** and **screensavers**
◆ interactive **games**
◆ canine **quizzes**
The **Smart Owner's Guide** series and **Club APBT** are backed by the experts at DOG FANCY magazine and DogChannel.com, who have been providing trusted and up-to-date information about dogs and dog people for 40 years. Log on and join the club today!

commitments while providing a loving home for your pit bull will help you raise a dog you can be proud of.

Allan Reznik
Editor-at-Large, DOG FANCY

A GOOD DOG

The American Pit Bull Terrier likes nothing better than to please his people. That willingness to please is no accident. Although the APBT's forebears were bred to fight other animals, they also were bred to willingly go to extremes to please their humans. Today, this eagerness makes the APBT surprisingly easy to train. Moreover, the breed's love of people can extend well beyond his immediate family.

That said, American Pit Bull Terriers are not pushovers. Although they love their people and want to please them, they may have their own ideas on how to do so — and sometimes those ideas conflict with those of their humans. Sometimes they can have a stubborn streak, but as a whole, American Pit Bull Terriers simply want to do what their master asks.

Different breeds have held the title of "dangerous dog" throughout history. In the 19th century, it was the Bloodhound. In the 1960s and 1970s, Doberman Pinschers and German Shepherd Dogs found themselves in the "dangerous dog" spotlight. The pit bull's turn came in the late 1980s, when *Sports Illustrated* plastered a photo of a snarling dog on its July 27, 1987 cover with the headline "Beware of This Dog." The story inside was about pit bulls and the widespread problem of dog fighting.

it's a **Fact**

Carol Gaines, a long-time APBT breeder and judge from Battle Ground, Wash., agrees. "They can be hard-headed and stubborn, but it's because they seem to think all the time," she says. "Labs are trainable, but APBTs are always busy training you. They are very happy when they make you happy; however, they want to do it their own way."

PHYSICAL CHARACTERISTICS

The pit bull is not an especially large dog. In fact, in his working form, the pit bull is a rather small dog. This enables owners to keep a pit bull in a small home or apartment quite comfortably. While he is an energetic dog when given the chance to exercise, he is a breed that prefers to relax when at home. As such, he will not be in the way at all times and will not make himself more conspicuous than many owners prefer their dogs to be.

The pit bull also tends to be a hardy dog. He can play hard and live long without costing his owner a fortune in veterinary bills.

The closer a line of pit bulls is to its original working stock, the hardier the dogs will be. It is not the least bit unusual to own a pit bull for 12, 13 or 14 years, or even more. When such dogs finally succumb to old age, they tend to do it without suffering long, protracted, painful and expensive illnesses.

PERSONALITY POINTS

Above all, the pit bull is an incredibly devoted dog. The breed becomes highly attached to his human family as long as he feels welcome at home as part of that family. As an extension of this attribute, a pit bull can also be a protective dog; and, a powerful and protective — yet small and convenient — dog can be very useful in the hands of responsible owners. However, unlike many very devoted dogs, the pit bull *can* accept change. Should the unfortunate situation arise when a family must give up its pet pit bull, the dog will become dedicated to his new owner with time. Therefore, a rescued pit bull may be a sound option for you to consider, particularly if you are familiar with the dog's previous owners and their living situation.

Most of all, the pit bull is a fine companion dog. Those who know the breed will often tell you that, in their opinion, there can be no finer companion dog than the pit bull. He is a dog who will bond to his entire human family, but one who will always hold a special place in his heart for the person he decides is his closest friend. He is a dog who will always be there for his owner. He is a forgiving breed, an exceedingly loyal breed, a fun-loving breed and a lifelong friend.

VERSATILITY OF THE BREED

We have accepted unabashedly the fact that the pit bull as a breed is the most adept

Did You Know?

Inspirational author and lecturer **Helen Keller** was accompanied by a dog described as a pit bull.

American Pit Bull Terriers can be lovable and loving family pets in the hands of the right owners.

"game dog" ever to have been produced. We also know of the pit bull's utilization as a "catch dog."

Guard work and personal protection work are other areas in which the pit bull breed often excels. The pit bull generally makes a useful home guardian and personal protection dog, primarily because he is such a devoted and determined breed. He is not a dog who automatically protects the space he happens to be occupying or whoever happens to be holding his leash. Instead, the pit bull is a dog who will often defend due to a sense of devotion to his family and his family's property.

THE BEST HOME FOR A PIT BULL

Before getting into the question of where to get your pit bull pup, we should consider the question of what types of homes are most appropriate for the pit bull breed. It is all too common these days for authors of breed books to present their breed as being ideal for every home. This is not true in any case, especially in the case of the pit bull.

A pit bull puppy sure is cute, but keep in mind that he'll grow into a powerful adult. Training is a must!

The pit bull is an ideal dog for an adult family with older (14 years and above) children and with someone at home most of the time. The size of the home is not as important; it can be large, with a fenced yard, or small. It can even be an apartment in the city. The important thing is that someone is home often and willing to take the dog on regular, long walks. This describes the best of all possible situations for the pit bull.

Conversely, the worst situation for a pit bull is one in which a dog is raised by a young person who, when the dog is older, becomes too busy to spend much time with him. Worse still is that this young person has children when the dog is grown and these children end up spending time with a dog who doesn't relate to them as true "members of the family." This is how so many of the pit bull disasters that we hear about in the media happen.

LAWS AGAINST DOGS

Breed-specific legislation refers to any law or statute that equates the qualities of a dangerous dog with a certain breed and bans or restricts certain breeds based on identity, not the behavior of a specific animal. BSL first came to light in 1980, when Hollywood, Fla., passed an ordinance requiring pit bull owners to register and prove they had $25,000 in liability insurance covering the dog's actions. In 1984, a New Mexico town went further, banning all pit bulls. Pit bulls in that town

could legally be confiscated and euthanized. Since that time, more than 100 communities have enacted BSLs.

Just as quickly as BSLs emerged, organizations formed to thwart it, adopting the unofficial mantra of "Punish the deed, not the breed." The Endangered Breed Association, American Dog Owners Association, American Veterinary Medical Association, American

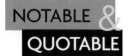

The number of pit bulls who cause trouble is statistically irrelevant. Media will have you believe that pit bulls are running rampant and attacking people. More people die every year from coconuts falling onto their heads than from pit bull attacks! We need perspective. — Mary Harwelik, a professional dog trainer and director of The Real Pit Bull Foundation in Garwood, N.J.

Kennel Club and various breed clubs all have taken positions against discriminating on the basis of breed. They contend that many other, non-restricted breeds are also responsible for serious attacks in which officers and media often misidentify dogs as belonging to restricted breeds, and that BSL violates the constitutional rights of affected dog owners.

Denver, Colo., is among the most hotly contested communities with BSL. Denver prohibits "any person to own, possess, keep, exercise control over, maintain, harbor, transport or sell within the city any pit bull." A pit bull is defined "any dog that is an American Pit Bull Terrier, American Staffordshire Terrier, Staffordshire Bull Terrier or any dog displaying the majority of physical traits of any one or more of the above breeds, or any dog exhibiting those distinguishing characteristics which substantially conform to the standards established by the American Kennel Club or United Kennel Club for any of the above breeds."

Statistics are also flawed by breed misidentification. With more than 700 breeds of dogs worldwide, the average person cannot identify even a small proportion of breeds. It's not uncommon for newspaper reporters and even animal-control officers to label Boxers, Shar-Peis, Dalmatians, Bullmastiffs and even Labrador Retrievers as pit bulls. When it comes to mixes, the situation becomes nearly impossible. Newspaper headlines mentioning "pit bull" attacks seem to elicit more interest than those reporting "dog" attacks, so there may be some motivation for the media to label any dangerous dog as a pit bull.

The expense in enforcing BSL has often been tremendous. A 2003 study conducted in Prince Georges County, Md., found that BSL cost them $560,000 over a two-year period, and that non-breed-specific parts of their animal-control code adequately covered every transgression responsible for serious dog bites.

Despite its costs in money, work hours and dogs, there's no evidence that BSL works. After the United Kingdom banned pit bulls in the 1990s, the number of pit bulls there plummeted, but the number of dog bites remained the same. In fact, no statistics exist that support the effectiveness of BSL.

Many dog organizations support dangerous dog control that is nondiscriminatory and enforceable. This includes strongly enforced leash laws, guidelines for dealing with dangerous dogs of any breed and increased public education to promote responsible dog ownership. Smart APBT owners can do their part to help pit bulls in a number of ways, including setting good examples, passing temperament tests, being involved in therapy work, talking to other dog owners and keeping abreast of legislation.

OWNER SUITABILITY

Being the perfect pit bull owner involves understanding your dog and complying with certain breed demands, but it also involves selecting this breed because it fits into your lifestyle. For example, if you own another dog and you know that your dogs will be unattended for a few hours each day, the pit bull may simply be the wrong breed for you. After all, fighting between your pit bull and other dogs you may meet on the street is easily discouraged. However, leaving two dogs alone for hours at a time, on a regular basis, with one of the two being a pit bull,

Everyone who owns this breed needs to realize that they are responsible for what happens with this breed, whether they like it or not. If you have a social, well-mannered and trained pit bull, get her out where the public can see her, even if you just take her for a walk to the coffee shop. If your dog is not social, well-mannered or in your control, take steps to get her that way!

— Kris Crawford, founder of For Pits' Sake Inc. in Los Gatos, Calif.

may be too much to ask of this breed. We must understand that when all is said and done, the pit bull was originally created to be a fighting dog.

If you are a working person or half of a working couple and you desire a pet that you can leave alone all day, almost every day, a dog of any breed is really the wrong pet for you. There will be other times in your life when you are ready for a dog, but this is not the right time.

Even if you are a person who simply hates to take a walk on a regular basis, the pit bull will be the wrong breed for you. There are other breeds that can live in such an environment. You would be doing both yourself and the pit bull breed a favor if you would select one of those breeds instead.

The perfect owner for an American Pit Bull Terrier is one who will return the devotion the dog will provide him. This owner will want the dog primarily for the fantastic companionship he will offer and not for the image he will exude. This owner will enjoy the exercise the pit bull demands as much as his dog will. This owner will understand the reputation by which the pit bull has become victimized and work to improve it. This owner will be in a position to take on a dog that may be with him for 15 years, without expecting the dog to deal with excessive change in his life. This owner will be one who can provide a very regular routine in all respects for his beloved pit bull.

If you are this person, the American Pit Bull Terrier may be a better choice from other purebred dogs than you may formerly have thought.

Are pit bulls OK with children? Just ask the Little Rascals, whose mascot Petey was an APBT!

Pop Pups

They are heroes in every sense of the word.

A World War I era American propaganda poster depicted rival nations with their national dogs dressed in military uniforms. Representing the United States was an American Pit Bull Terrier. The caption below read, "I'm neutral but not afraid of any of them."

The real-life embodiment of the dog on that poster was a stray pit bull found by Pvt. John Conroy on the Yale University campus in 1917. Conroy, who was training for deployment to the European front, named the dog Stubby. Along with the other trainees, Stubby learned to salute, putting his right paw to his eyebrow, and became familiar with bugle calls and drill marching routines. The dog was so beloved as a mascot that he was granted permission to remain with Conroy and traveled to battle front lines with the 102nd Infantry Division. He repaid his adopters by warning them of an oncoming gas attack, thus saving the platoon, and capturing a German spy. As a reward, the commander put Stubby in for a promotion to the rank of sergeant, making him the first pit bull to be given rank in the U.S. armed forces. Sgt. Stubby served in 17 battles and was wounded twice in action!

Another popular World War I era pit bull was Pig, who called the University of Texas at Austin home. Pig went to classes with students, attended athletic events and participated in morning "fall outs" with military aeronautics cadets.

One of the most famous American Pit Bull Terriers was Petey, who starred in the *Our Gang* comedies of the 1930s with the Little Rascals. He was also registered with the AKC as an American Staffordshire Terrier.

Weela, a pit bull, was named the Ken-L Ration Dog Hero in 1993 for exhibiting bravery in saving 30 people, 29 dogs, 13 horses and a cat during heavy floods in Southern California.

Another hero was Dixie Butler, a pit bull from Georgia who protected her family's children from a water moccasin. Dixie placed herself between the snake and the children, suffering multiple bites to her face and eyes. Happily, Dixie fully recovered and was inducted into the Georgia Animal Hall of Fame in 1999.

Pit bulls Cheyenne, Dakota and Tahoe, owned by Kristine Crawford, work full time as search-and-rescue dogs for the Alameda County Sheriff Canine Search and Rescue Unit in Castro Valley, Calif. They spread their message of safety and tail wagging through a variety of other programs as well. For one, they participate in a youth outreach program called Hug-a-Tree, which teaches kids what to do if they are lost in the wilderness. In animal-assisted therapy, Crawford and her dogs go into hospitals and family shelters. "The visits achieve lower heart rates, [they] calm disturbed children [and] get uncommunicative people to talk," Crawford says.

The American Pit Bull Terrier is a pure-bred, but many pit bull mixes exist.

THE PIT BULL PROFILE

Energy, excitement and loyalty — all in one neat package!

COUNTRY OF ORIGIN: United States

WHAT HIS FRIENDS CALL HIM: Yankee Terrier, pit bull, APBT, Half and Half, American Bull Terrier

SIZE: 18 to 22 inches; 35 to 60 pounds

COAT & COLOR: The pit bull's coat is smooth and can come in any color or color combination, except merle (a bluish or reddish gray mixed with splotches of black)

PERSONALITY TRAITS: These dogs are known to be confident, fun-loving and have a strong zest for life.

WITH KIDS: The APBT is friendly with children.

WITH OTHER PETS: They often act aggressive towards other dogs, especially those of the same sex.

ENERGY LEVEL: high

EXERCISE NEEDS: Daily exercise is very important.

GROOMING NEEDS: regular brushing, but they are overall relatively low maintenance

TRAINING NEEDS: APBTs enjoy obedience training and learning new things. Because of their high energy, these dogs need to be kept busy to keep out of trouble.

LIVING ENVIRONMENT: This dog gets along well with a dog-experienced individual or family. They can thrive in a city, country or suburban setting.

LIFESPAN: 10 to 12 years

CHAPTER 7

ALL-AMERICAN

DOG

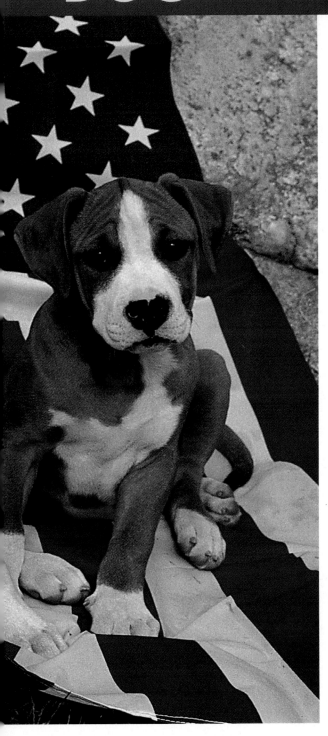

Americans like to think of the pit bull, or more properly, the American Pit Bull Terrier, as being a breed of purely American origin. To a large extent, this is true. After all, it was in the United States that this breed took on its definitive form, ability and character.

As there are no written records that clearly document the origin of the American Pit Bull Terrier, disagreement among its advocates abounds. Most American pit bull historians feel that the American Pit Bull Terrier is the American expression of the game-bred Stafford or Staffordshire Bull Terrier of the United Kingdom. These breed fanciers maintain that as English, and especially Irish, immigrants to the United States established themselves throughout America, the little dogs they prized so highly at home — the game-bred Staffords — sometimes traveled with them. Separated from their foundation stock, the gene pool of Staffordshire Bull Terriers in the United States became more distinct and was subject to the changes imposed by the thinking of American dog breeders, the most obvious of these changes being an increase in the pit bull's size.

Did You Know?

The American Pit Bull Terrier can be any color or color combination other than merle (a bluish or reddish gray mixed with splotches of black), according to the United Kennel Club breed standard.

Other pit bull fanciers have a different opinion regarding the origin of the breed. These fanciers feel that the pit bull is a modern-day expression of the original English Bulldog. They speculate that, unlike the Staffordshire Bull Terrier, a breed of known bull-and-terrier ancestry, the APBT has no terrier blood in him at all, but rather is a continuation of the pure Bulldog of Elizabethan days. They further speculate that the very obvious differences between the modern show dog known as the Bulldog and the pit bull reflect the vastly different purposes for which each was bred: showing versus working.

Bobbie Morehouse of Haddam, Conn., an American Pit Bull Terrier breeder and American Temperament Test Society tester, believes the terrier influence in the American Pit Bull Terrier is a strong one. "In my opinion, the true APBT is a complex balance of these two distinct types, the Bulldog and the terrier," Morehouse says. "This will always be a controversy because it is human nature to see and believe what one wants to see in their dogs, but a dog with a very obvious Bulldog-like appearance will almost always reveal his terrier traits upon close examination, and more terrier-like dogs will also reveal their underlying Bulldog influence. You just have to look."

FIGHTING PAST

The specifics of ancient breed history, and the breed's modern reputation notwithstanding, show that there can be no doubt about one thing, and that one thing is the core function of the pit bull breed. Throughout the entire existence of the breed, from its earliest days and, to some extent, through modern times, the pit bull in his purest working form has been and remains essentially a fighting dog. This is to say that the breed's function,

it's a Fact

In 1970, the American Dog Owner's Association formed to eliminate dog fighting for good, and those who want to protect pit bulls and other dogs from the abuses of the fighting ring continue to work to eliminate this cruel and illegal sport.

The pit bull is a classic American symbol — as classic as riding a shiny, black motorcycle through America's heartland.

his very purpose was — and in the minds of some, remains — to be a gambler's tool.

The breed was originally selectively bred without regard for looks, but rather only for his ever-increasing ability to fight other pit bulls, and only pit bulls, in drawn out combat events that took place in manmade dog pits for the enjoyment of human spectators. Note that, unlike some breeds, the pit bull's purpose was never to attack man. In fact, it must be noted here that in the organized combat events for which the pit bull was and occasionally still is used, these dogs are handled by their owners throughout the event. Those who use these dogs in such events have no use for a dog that would in any way endanger the handler rather than his canine opponent.

AMERICAN-MADE

The American Pit Bull Terrier and the American Staffordshire Terrier developed in much the same way as bull breeds did in England. People immigrating to the United States brought their dogs with them in the 1700s and throughout the 1800s. The dogs shared the work of the people they came with, working as catch dogs and farm dogs to drive semiwild cattle and hogs and hauling carts for miners.

Just as in the motherland, early American life included bullbaiting and dog-fighting, and on Friday and Saturday nights, working men would match their dogs in the pits and gamble on them. These types of dogs — which went by numerous names, including pit terriers, pit bull terriers, half and halfs, Staffordshire fighting dogs, old family dogs, Yankee terriers (in the North) and Rebel terriers (in the South) — became today's American Pit Bull Terrier, American Staffordshire Terrier and American Bulldog.

BECOMING LEGIT

In 1898, the United Kennel Club was formed, solely for the purpose of registering American Pit Bull Terriers. The first APBT registered, Bennett's Ring, belonged to Chauncey Bennett, founder of the UKC. A little more than a decade later, the American Dog Breeders Association formed to register APBTs. The ADBA was founded by Guy McCord, a friend of John P. Colby, which is a grand name in the realm of American Pit Bull Terriers.

"The Colbys have bred APBTs for generations," says Cindy Cooke, vice president of dog events for the UKC in Kalamazoo, Mich. "Of course, their dogs were originally fighters. There are pictures of Mr. Colby with his fighting dogs. They were world-famous, and they're still breeding them today."

Pit bull advocacy groups are always short-handed and appreciate any help they can get. Remember, these dogs don't have a voice of their own and need breed supporters to speak up for them. Donating money to rescue groups is one way of helping, as is volunteering your time to take care of the dogs, or bringing a foster dog into your home until she can find a place to call her permanent home.

THE AKC'S PIT BULL

As dog fighting was becoming illegal in the United States, some owners of APBTs wanted to legitimize the breed and distance it from its fighting roots.

Also during this time, an American cinema series by the name of *Our Gang* (or *The Little Rascals*) featured among its regular cast of characters a pit bull by the name of "Petey," also known as "Pete the Pup." The popularity of the series and its canine mascot brought such positive attention to the breed that by 1936, the prestigious American Kennel Club began to register the pit bull. Unhappy with the name of the breed, however, those responsible for registry of the breed with the AKC decided to change the breed's official name to Staffordshire Terrier and eventually to American Staffordshire Terrier many years later.

During the late 1930s, the pit bulls being registered by the United Kennel Club, the American Dog Breeders Association and the American Kennel Club were all the same breed with exactly the same physique. Indeed breeders, such as John P. Colby, registered their dogs both as American Pit Bull Terriers with the UKC and as American Staffordshire Terriers with the AKC.

According to the American Staffordshire Terrier Club of America, although ancestors of the AmStaff were fighting dogs, selective breeding since the 1930s has moved away from the fighting heritage. Today's AmStaff is a companion and show dog rather than a blood-hungry gladiator.

Pit bulls, too, have taken their talents to less violent arenas of competition. Pit bulls are versatile dogs who compete successfully in conformation, obedience, tracking, agility, protection work and weight pulling.

APBT vs. AST: What's the Difference?

Some people say the American Pit Bull Terrier and the American Staffordshire Terrier are the same breed. Others say no way. What's the truth? That depends on who you ask.

"I believe the American Pit Bull Terrier and the American Staffordshire Terrier are the same breed because all the AKC-registered American Staffordshire Terriers were bred down directly from the United Kennel Club-registered American Pit Bull Terriers," says Bobbie Morehouse of Haddam, Conn., a member of the National American Pit Bull Terrier Association. "The most compelling argument for this would be the fact that a dog today can be both a UKC-registered American Pit Bull Terrier and an AKC-registered American Staffordshire Terrier."

True, no other breeds have been introduced into either breed to distinguish them, but many American Staffordshire Terrier breeders assert that despite a common ancestry, the breeds today are different. The American Staffordshire Terrier has a smaller gene pool and is more likely to look consistent. According to Morehouse, because more people breed American Pit Bull Terriers for more reasons, they are more likely to vary in size and appearance. "That's for better or worse, depending on your perspective," Morehouse says. "I personally hold a great deal of reverence for the APBT's diversity, and her well-deserved recognition as an exceptional working dog."

As for the written breed standards, they look similar, too. The UKC standard for the APBT specifies an ideal weight between 30 to 65 pounds, but doesn't specify height. The AKC standard for the American Staffordshire Terriers specifies a height of 17 to 19 inches, and that "height and weight should be in proportion."

The American Pit Bull Terrier can be any color other than merle, according to the UKC breed standard, while the American Staffordshire Terrier can be any color at all; although all-white dogs or dogs more than 80 percent white, as well as black and tan and liver, are "not to be encouraged." Otherwise, the differences tend to be based more on fashion and individual breeder preferences than anything else. Are they the same? You decide!

In temperament and appearance, the modern APBT and the AmStaff are identical, says Cooke. "Probably half of our APBTs registered with the UKC are also registered with the AKC as American Staffordshire Terriers," she says. "All the AKC AmStaffs are descended from the same dogs as the UKC APBTs. The only difference in the standards is that the AKC for some reason did not accept the red nose."

TO MODERN TIMES

The popularity of the pit bull, with his various registries and with his many official breed names, waned during the 1940s and onward until the mid-1970s. However, the breed was never threatened with extinction. It never reached a condition in which one could say there was no interest in these dogs at all, but other breeds became the focus of the average dog fancier's attention.

Also during this period, the pit bull in both his working form and his show form, and regardless of how he was registered, enjoyed a condition of relative obscurity. He lived in peace in America. No one thought a pit bull to be a dangerous dog. Many forgot what a pit bull even was. Those who remembered the breed recalled the dog fondly from the comedy series on television. The reputation for being dangerous was then reserved for such breeds as the Doberman Pinscher. The pit bull was left to his fanciers almost exclusively.

At about the time that the reputation of the pit bull breed began to change for the worse in the United States (about 1980), Dutch dog fighters had developed an interest in these dogs. The first pit bulls to find their way to Holland were serious "match dogs" acquired from hard-core American "dog men." It was not long before "underground" dog fighters in the United States began to take notice of the serious matches and breeding being conducted in Holland. From Holland, interest in the pit bull spread to Germany, the United Kingdom, France, Italy, parts of Scandinavia and elsewhere in Europe and throughout the world.

By the late 1980s or about 1990, the "dangerous pit bull" saga began to spread over the American borders to other, and even far off, countries. Following a lead established by law enforcement officials in Britain, countries began to pass laws against the ownership and importation of this breed that had been largely unknown, even in its homeland, only a few years before.

Fanciers blame the media for sensationalizing the breed and printing dog-fighting pictures that made pit bulls look vicious and

Because the American Pit Bull Terrier was considered the 'poor man's breed,' he had to earn his keep and provide a valuable service. This was a contributing factor to the breed's range of types and characteristics. — Bobbie Morehouse of Haddam, Conn., an American Pit Bull Terrier breeder, exhibitor and competitor

terrifying. This attracted criminals and people who wanted a pit bull to look tough, as well as those still engaged in illegal dog fighting. But many believe that bad-guy image is misplaced because people confuse animal aggression with aggression toward humans. "A pit bull is not a guardian breed like a Rottweiler or a Doberman," says Janie Collins, a UKC dog show judge. "They should never be aggressive toward humans. It's not a characteristic of this breed."

BREED BANS

Their fighting heritage has cost pit bulls dearly, despite the fact that many are model citizens. Germany banned bully breeds after a pit bull and another mixed breed dog belonging to a drug dealer killed a child, Cooke says. Some bully breeds are outlawed in England, their home country, as well. And many cities in the United States have developed or are considering ordinances that would ban specific breeds, including bully breeds.

Cooke is not sanguine about their future. "The bully breeds are the miner's canary in our battle with [extreme] animal rights people," she says. "They have successfully used the media to demonize these dogs. If we do not stand up and fight for their continued right to exist, pit bulls will eventually disappear."

Did You Know?

Dog parks are great places for dogs to mingle, play and chase one another. **But they're not a good place for APBTs.** That's because dog parks are also a great place for fights to break out. Several dogs start chasing one dog, one dog yelps or a couple of dogs just take a dislike to each other, and suddenly every dog is piling on. Unfortunately, whether your APBT starts it or not, this is what he was bred to do, and chances are he's not going to stop until the other dog is severely injured or dead.

THE BULLY

As rough and tumble as the American Pit Bull Terrier can be, nothing is cuter than a pit bull puppy. Their sweet faces and round little bodies inspire *oohs* and *ahhs* from all who see them. That wonderful endearing quality, however, can also distract you from taking the time and doing the legwork necessary to find a puppy who's not only adorable, but healthy in body and temperament as well. The key to finding the best APBT puppy for you is to resist being charmed into a hasty decision and wait to find a responsible breeder. Then, have fun picking just the right puppy from a litter of those lovable faces.

You're going to have your pit bull for 12 to 15 years, so the time you spend early on to locate a healthy, well-adjusted puppy from a reputable breeder will definitely pay off for you in the long run. Look for a dedicated and ethical breeder who values good health and stable personalities, and one who really cares what happens to the dog for the rest of his life spent with you.

Testosterone increases aggression. Most fatal dog attacks are carried out by intact (unneutered) males. With few exceptions, your life — and your dog's life — will be much easier if you neuter him before sexual maturity. Even females can become more tractable when spayed, as some females tend to be more aggressive according to their estrus (heat) cycle.

it's a
Fact

Why is this so important? "This is a breed with a unique personality who needs to be bred correctly by someone with experience who really knows what he or she is doing," says Valerie Piltz, vice president of the National American Pit Bull Terrier Association. "If not, you may wind up with a dog who's overly aggressive, has a ton of health problems and doesn't even look like an American Pit Bull Terrier."

Be sure to avoid puppy mills and backyard breeders. Puppy mills are large-scale breeding operations that produce puppies in an assembly-line fashion without regard to health and socialization. Backyard breeders are typically well-meaning, regular pet owners who simply do not possess enough knowledge about their breed and breeding to produce healthy puppies.

The United Kennel Club provides a list of breeders in good standing with the organization. Visit their website for more information: www.ukcdogs.com

EVALUATING BREEDERS

Once you have the names and numbers of breeders in your area, start contacting them to find out more about their breeding programs. But, before you pick up the phone, plan to ask the questions that will get you the information you need to know.

Prospective buyers interview breeders much the same way that a

Choose a reputable breeder and you'll get a well-socialized puppy.

breeder should interview a buyer. Make a list of questions and record the answers so that you can compare them to the answers from other breeders whom you may interview later. The right questions are those that help you identify who has been in the breed a respectable number of years and who is actively showing their dogs. Ask in-depth questions regarding the genetic health of the parents, grandparents and great grandparents of any puppy you are considering. Ask what sort of genetic testing program the breeder adheres to.

A prospective buyer should look to see if a breeder actively shows his or her dogs. Showing indicates that the breeder is bringing out examples from his or her breeding program for the public to see. If there are any obvious problems, such as temperament or general conformation, they will be readily apparent. Also, the main reason to breed dogs is to improve the quality of the breed. If the breeder is not showing, then he or she is

If a breeder advertises or tells you that their stock has an extra-large head size, is a rare color, weighs 80 pounds or more, is good for protection or provides stud service, run the other way. None of these claims describe what a purebred American Pit Bull Terrier is all about, and it's usually an excuse to ask for more money. Take the time to learn about the breed before you contemplate buying or adopting one. — Valerie Piltz, vice president, the National American Pit Bull Terrier Association

Puppies learn to speak "dog" from their siblings, so be sure your breeder doesn't let you bring home your puppy before at minimum 8 weeks of age.

more likely breeding purely for the monetary aspect and may have less concern for the welfare and future of the breed.

Smart potential puppy buyers inquire about health and determine the breeder's willingness to work with them in the future. The prospective buyer should see what kind of health guarantees the breeder gives. You should also find out if the breeder will be available for future consultation regarding the dog, and find out if the

breeder will take the dog back if something unforeseen happens.

Prospective buyers should ask plenty of questions, and in return, buyers should also be prepared to answer questions posed by a responsible breeder who wants to make sure their pit bull puppy is going to a good home. Be prepared for a battery of questions from the breeder regarding your purpose for wanting an American Pit Bull Terrier and whether or not you can properly care for one. Avoid buying from a breeder who does little or no screening. If breeders don't ask questions, they are not concerned with where their pit bull puppies end up. In this case, the dogs' best interests are probably not the breeder's motive for breeding. You should find a breeder who is willing to answer any questions you have and is knowledgeable about the history of the breed, health issues and about the background of their own dogs. Learn about a breeder's long-term commitment to the breed and to their puppies after they leave the kennel.

Look for a breeder who knows their purpose for producing a particular litter, one who is knowledgeable in the pedigrees of their dogs and of the breed itself, and has had the necessary health screenings performed on the parents. The breeder should also be asking you for references if they are interested in establishing a relationship with you in consideration for a puppy. If after one phone conversation with a breeder, the person is supplying you with an address in which to send a deposit, continue your search for a reputable breeder elsewhere.

CHOOSING THE RIGHT PUP

Once you have found a breeder you are comfortable with, your next step is to pick the right puppy for you. The good news is that if you have done your homework in finding a responsible breeder, you can count on this person to give you plenty of help in choosing the right pup for your personality and lifestyle. In fact, most good breeders will recommend a specific puppy to a buyer once they know what kind of dog the buyer wants.

After you have narrowed down the search and selected a reputable breeder, rely on the experience of the breeder to help you select the exact puppy. The selection of the puppy depends a lot on what purpose the pup is being purchased for. If the pup is being purchased as a show prospect, the breeder will offer their assessment of the pups who meet this criteria and be able to explain the strengths and faults of each pup.

Whether your pup is show- or pet-quality, a good, stable temperament is vital for a happy relationship. Generally, you want to avoid a timid puppy or one who is very dominant. Temperament is very important, and a reputable breeder should spend a lot of time with the pups and be able to offer an evaluation of each pup's personality.

JOIN OUR ONLINE
Club APBT®

Questions to Expect
Be prepared for the breeder to ask you some questions, too.

This isn't a steadfast rule, and some breeders only insist on meeting the children to see how they handle puppies. It all depends on the breeder.

1. Have you previously owned an American Pit Bull Terrier?
The breeder is trying to gauge how familiar you are with the breed. If you have never owned one, illustrate your knowledge of APBTs by telling the breeder about your research.

2. Do you have children? What are their ages?
Some breeders are wary about selling a dog to families with younger children.

3. How long have you wanted an American Pit Bull Terrier?
This helps a breeder know if this purchase is an impulse buy, or a carefully thought-out decision. Buying on impulse is one of the biggest mistakes owners can make. Be patient.

Join Club APBT to get a complete list of questions a breeder should ask you. Click on "Downloads" at: **DogChannel.com/Club-APBT**

Reputable breeders should tell each buyer which puppy is appropriate for their home situation and personalities. They may not allow you to choose the puppy, although they will certainly take your preference into consideration.

Some breeders, on the other hand, believe it's important for you to have a strong involvement in picking a puppy from the litter. Louis Colby, an American Pit Bull Terrier breeder in Newburyport, Mass., lets his puppy buyers make the decision on which pup to take home. "Not everyone is looking for the same things in a dog," Colby says. "Some people want a quiet, laidback attitude. Others want an outgoing, active dog. When pups are old enough to go to their new homes at roughly 8 to 12 weeks of age, we prefer you make your own decision because no one can tell at this age which pup will make the most intelligent or affectionate dog. The color, sex and markings are obvious, but that is about all you can tell for sure at this age. Everything else being equal — size, health, etc. — we suggest picking the pup that you have a gut feeling for."

Chemistry between buyer and puppy is important and should play a role in determining which pup goes to which home. When possible, make numerous visits, and in effect, let a puppy choose you. There will usually be one puppy who spends more time with a buyer and is more comfortable relaxing and sitting with or on a person.

With the popularity of American Pit Bull Terriers, shelters and rescue groups across the country are often inundated with sweet, loving examples of the breed — from the tiniest puppies to senior dogs,

petite females to blocky males. Often, to get the pit bull of your dreams, it takes just a journey to the local shelter. Or perhaps you could find your ideal dog waiting patiently in the arms of a foster parent at a nearby rescue group. It just takes a bit of effort, patience and a willingness to find the right dog for your family — not just the cutest dog on the block.

The perks of owning an American Pit Bull Terrier are plentiful: companionship, unconditional love, true loyalty and laughter, just to name a few. So why choose the adoption option? Because you literally are saving a life!

Owners of adopted dogs swear they're more grateful and loving than any dog they've owned before. It's almost as if they knew what dire fate awaited them and are so thankful to you. Pit bulls, known for their people-pleasing personalities, seem to embody this mentality whole-heartedly when they're rescued. And they want to give something back.

Another perk: Almost all adopted dogs come fully vetted, with proper medical treatment, vaccinations, medicine, as well as being spayed or neutered. Some are even licensed and microchipped.

Don't disregard older dogs, thinking the only good pair-up is you and a puppy. Adult APBTs are more established behaviorally and personality-wise, helping to better mesh their characteristics with yours in this game of matchmaker. Puppies are always high in demand, so if you open your options to include adult dogs, you'll have a better chance of adopting quickly. Plus, adult dogs are often housetrained, more calm, chew-proof and don't need to be taken outside in the middle of the night. Five times. In the pouring rain.

The National American Pit Bull Terrier Association offers rescue support information (www.napbta.com) or log onto Petfinder.com (www.petfinder.com). The site's searchable database enables you to find a pit bull puppy in your area who needs a break in the form of a compassionate owner like you. More websites are listed in the Resources chapter on page 166.

CHECKING FOR APBT QUALITIES

Whether you are dealing with a breeder who wants to pick a pup for you or lets you make the decision alone, consider certain points when evaluating the pup that you may end up calling your own. The pup should be friendly and outgoing, not skittish in any way. He should be forgiving of correction. He shouldn't be too terribly mouthy. The pup should readily follow you and be willing to snuggle in your lap and be turned onto his back easily without a problem.

Proper temperament is important. A pit bull puppy who has a dominant personality requires an experienced owner who will be firm during training. A puppy who is a little shy requires heavy socialization to build his confidence.

Evaluate each puppy's temperament on your own, with the breeder's permission. The temperament of the pups can be evaluated by spending some time watching them. If you can visit the pups and observe them first together with their littermates, then you can see how they interact with each other.

You may be able to pinpoint which ones are the bullies and which ones are more submissive. In general, look for a puppy who is more interested in you than in his littermates. Then, take each pup individually to a new location away from the rest of the litter. Put the pup down on the ground, walk away and see how he reacts away from the security of his littermates. The pup may be afraid at first, but should gradually recover and start checking out the new surroundings.

D-I-Y TEMPERAMENT TEST

Puppies come in a wide assortment of temperaments to suit just about everyone. If you are looking for a dog who is easily trainable and a good companion to your family, you most likely want a dog with a medium temperament.

Temperament testing can help you determine the type of disposition your potential puppy possesses. A pup with a medium, trainable temperament will have the following reactions to these various tests, best conducted when the pup is about 7 weeks.

Breeder Q&A

Here are some questions *you* should ask a breeder and the preferred answers you want.

Q. How often do you have litters available?

A. The answer you want to hear is "occasionally" or "once or twice a year." A breeder who doesn't have litters all that often is probably more concerned with the quality of his puppies, rather than making money.

Q. What kinds of health problems have you had with your American Pit Bull Terriers?

A. Beware of a breeder who says, "none." Every breed has health issues. For APBTs, some health problems include chronic hip dysplasia, luxated patella and demodectic mange.

Get a complete list of questions to ask an APBT breeder — and the correct answers — on Club APBT. Log onto **DogChannel.com/Club-APBT** and click on "Downloads."

Step 1. To test a pit bull pup's social attraction to humans and his confidence or shyness in approaching them, coax him toward you by kneeling down and clapping your hands gently. A puppy with a medium temperament will come readily, tail up or tail down.

Step 2. To test a pup's eagerness to follow, walk away from him while he is watching you. The pup should readily follow you, tail up.

Step 3. To see how a pit bull pup handles restraint, kneel down and roll the pup gently on his back. Using a light but firm touch, hold him in this position with one hand for 30 seconds. The pup should settle down after some initial struggle and offer some or steady eye contact.

Step 4. To evaluate a pup's level of social dominance, stand up, then crouch down beside the pup and stroke him from head to back. A pup with a medium temperament, neither too dominant nor too submissive,

should cuddle up to you and lick your face, or squirm and lick your hands.

Step 5. An additional test of a pup's dominance is to bend over, cradle him under his belly with your fingers interlaced and palms up, and elevate him just off the ground. Hold for 30 seconds. He should not struggle and should be relaxed, or he should struggle and then settle down and lick you.

Did You Know?

Properly bred puppies come from parents who were selected based upon their genetic disease profile. Their mothers should have been vaccinated, free of all internal and external parasites, and properly nourished. For these reasons, a visit to the veterinarian who cared for the mother is recommended. The mother can pass on disease resistance to her puppies, which can last for 8 to 10 weeks.

Food intolerance is the inability of the dog to completely digest certain foods. Puppies who have done very well on their mother's milk may not do well on cow's milk. The result of this food intolerance may be loose bowels, passing gas and stomach pains. These are the only obvious symptoms of food intolerance, and that makes diagnosis difficult.

A HEALTHY PUPPY

To assess a puppy's health, take a deliberate, thorough look at each part of his body. A healthy puppy has bright eyes, a healthy coat, a good appetite and firm stool.

Watch for a telltale link between physical and mental health. A healthy pit bull, as with any breed of puppy, will display a happier, more positive attitude than an unhealthy puppy. A pup's belly should not be over extended or hard, as this may be a sign of worms. Also, if you are around the litter long enough to witness a bowel movement, the stool should be solid, and the pup should not show any signs of discomfort. Look into the pup's eyes, too. They should be bright and full of life.

When purchasing a puppy, buyers hear from breeders that these dogs are just like any other puppy — times 10! They are very smart, calculating, stubborn and often have their own agendas. If prospective owners aren't willing to spend a fair amount of time with a pit bull, then the breed is not for them. This bully breed wants to be with people more than other dogs and is quite like a 7-year-old boy in that he needs attention and consistent reinforcement for behavioral parameters. Once through adolescence, however, an American Pit Bull Terrier is the best friend, guardian and companion a person or family could have.

PUPPY PARTICULARS

Here are signs to look for when picking a puppy from a breeder. When in doubt, ask the breeder which puppy they think has the best personality/temperament to fit your lifestyle.

1. Look at the area where the pups spend most of their time. It is OK if they play

For a happy, healthy adult, you must begin training and socialization as a pup; that means finding a breeder who has already begun doing both before you take your puppy home.

outdoors part of the day, but they should sleep indoors at night so that the pups can interact with people and become accustomed to hearing ordinary household noises. This builds a solid foundation for a secure, well-socialized puppy. The puppy area should be clean, well lit, have fresh drinking water and interesting toys.

2. Sure, you're only buying one puppy, but make sure to see all of the puppies in the litter. By 5 weeks of age, healthy pups will begin playing with one another and should be lively and energetic. It's OK if they're asleep when you visit, but stay long enough to see them wake up. Once they're up, they shouldn't be lethargic or weak, as this may be a sign of illness.

3. Pups should be confident and eager to greet you. A pup who is shy or fearful and stays in the corner may be sick or insecure. Although some introverted pups come out of their shells later on, many do not. These dogs will always be fearful as adults and are not good choices for an active, noisy family with or without children, or for people who have never had a dog. These dogs frighten easily and will require a tremendous amount of training and socialization in order to live a happy life.

Choose a pup who is happy and eager to interact with you but reject the one who is either too shy or too bossy. These temperament types are a challenge to deal with, and require a lot of training to socialize. The perfect APBT puppy personality is somewhere between the two extremes.

4. If it's feeding time during your visit, all pups should be eager to gobble up their food. Refusing to eat may signal illness.

5. The dog's skin should be smooth, clean and shiny without any sores or bumps. Puppies should not be biting or scratching at themselves continuously, which could be a sign of fleas.

6. After 10 to 12 days, their eyes should be open and clear without any redness or discharge. Pups should not scratch at their eyes, this may cause an infection or signal irritation.

7. Vomiting or coughing more than once is not normal. The pup may be ill and should visit the veterinarian.

8. Visit long enough to see the pups eliminate. All stools should be firm without being watery or bloody. These are signs of illness or that a puppy has worms.

9. Pups should walk or run without limping.

10. A healthy puppy who eats enough should not be skinny. You should be able to slightly feel his ribs, but you should not be able to see the ribs.

BREEDER PAPERS

Everything today comes with an instruction manual. When you purchase an APBT, it's no different. A reputable breeder should give you a registration application; a sales contract; a health guarantee; the dog's complete health records; a three-, four- or five-generation pedigree; and some general information about behavior, care, conformation, health and training.

Signs of a Healthy Puppy
Here are a few things you should look for when selecting a puppy from a litter.

1. **NOSE:** It should be slightly moist to the touch, but there shouldn't be excessive discharge. The puppy should not be sneezing or sniffling persistently.

2. **SKIN AND COAT:** Your pit bull puppy's coat should be soft and shiny, without flakes or excessive shedding. Watch out for patches of missing hair, redness, bumps or sores. The pup

should have a pleasant smell. Check for parasites, such as fleas or ticks.

3. **BEHAVIOR:** A healthy APBT puppy may be sleepy, but he should not be lethargic. A healthy pup will be playful at times, not isolated in a corner. You should see occasional bursts of energy and interaction with littermates. When it's mealtime, a healthy pup will take an interest in his food.

There are more signs to look for when picking out the perfect pit bull puppy for you. Download the list at **DogChannel.com/Club-APBT**

Registration Application. This document from the United Kennel Club or the American Dog Breeders Association assigns your puppy a number and identifies the dog by listing his date of birth, the names of the parents and shows that he is registered as a purebred APBT. It doesn't prove whether or not your dog is a show- or a pet-quality pit bull and doesn't provide any health guarantee.

Sales Contract.

Reputable breeders discuss the terms of the contract before asking you to sign it. This is a written understanding of your expectations about the puppy and shows that the breeder cares about the puppy's welfare throughout his life. The contract can include such terms as requiring you to keep the dog indoors at night, spaying or neutering if the puppy is not going to be a show dog, providing routine veterinary care throughout the dog's life, and assurance that you'll feed your dog a healthy diet. Most responsible dog breeders will ask that you take your dog to obedience classes and earn a Canine Good Citizen title on him before 2 years of age. Many breeders also require new owners to have totally secure fencing and gates around their yard. American Pit Bull Terriers are incredible escape artists, and they will find a way out of the yard if there's even the slightest opening.

Health Guarantee. This includes a letter from a veterinarian that the puppy has been examined and is healthy, and states that the breeder will replace the dog if the pup develops a genetic, life-threatening illness during his lifetime.

Health Records. Here's everything you want to know about not only your puppy's health, but the parents', as well.

It should include the dates the puppy was vaccinated, dewormed and examined by a veterinarian for signs of heart murmur, plus the parents' test results for the presence or absence of hip and elbow dysplasia, heart problems and slipped patellas.

Pedigree. Breeders should give you a copy of the pit bull puppy's three-, four- or five-generation pedigree. Many have photos of the dog's ancestors they will proudly share with you.

Information. The best breeders pride themselves on handing over a notebook full of the latest information on APBT behavior, care, conformation, health and training. Be sure to read it because it will provide invaluable help while raising your dog.

ESSENTIALS

Don't for one second think that a pit bull would prefer to live in a place described as a pit or a barn! He, like every other breed, wants to live in the best accommodations with plenty of toys, soft bedding and other luxuries. Your home is now his home, too. And before you bring that new puppy or rescue dog into his new forever home, you need to make it accessible for him.

In fact, in order for him to grow into a stable, well-adjusted dog, he has to feel comfortable in his surroundings. Remember, he is leaving the warmth and security of his mother and littermates, as well as the familiarity of the only place he has ever known, so it is important to make his transition to your home — his new home — as easy as possible.

PUPPY-PROOFING

Aside from making sure that your APBT will be comfortable in your home, you also have to ensure that your home is safe, which means taking the proper precautions to keep your pup away from things that are dangerous for him.

> **it's a Fact**
>
> **Dangers lurk indoors and out.** Keep your curious pit bull from investigating your shed and garage. Antifreeze and fertilizers, such as those you would use for roses, will kill an APBT. Keep these items on high shelves that are out of reach from your dog.

A smart owner will puppy-proof the home inside and out before bringing their APBT home for the first time. Place breakables out of reach. If he is limited to certain places within the house, keep potentially dangerous items in off-limit areas. If your APBT is going to spend time in a crate, make sure that there is nothing near it he can reach if he sticks his curious little nose or paws through the openings.

The outside of your home must also be safe. Your pup will want to run and explore the yard, and he should be granted that freedom — as long as you are there to supervise him. Do not let a fence give you a false sense of security; you would be surprised how crafty (and persistent) a dog can be in figuring out how to dig under a fence or squeeze his way through small holes. The remedy is to make the fence well embedded into the ground. Be sure to repair or secure any gaps in the fence. Check the fence periodically to ensure that it is in good shape and make repairs as needed; a very determined pit bull pup may work on the same spot until he is able to get through.

The following are a few common problem areas smart pit bull owners watch out for in the home:

■ **Electrical cords and wiring:** No electrical cord or wiring is safe. Many office-supply stores sell products to keep wires gathered under desks, as well as products that prevent office chair wheels (and puppy teeth) from damaging electrical cords. If you have exposed cords and wires, these products aren't very expensive and can be used to keep a pup out of trouble.

■ **Trash cans:** Don't waste your time trying to train your pit bull not to get into the trash. Simply put the garbage behind a cabinet door and use a child-safe lock if necessary. Dogs love bathroom trash (i.e., cotton balls, cotton swabs, used razors, dental floss, etc.), all of which are extremely dangerous! Put this trash can in a cabinet under the sink and make sure you always shut the door to the bathroom.

■ **Household cleaners:** Make sure your American Pit Bull Terrier puppy doesn't have access to any of these deadly chemicals. Keep them behind closed cabinet doors, using child-safe locks if necessary.

■ **Pest control sprays and poisons:** Chemicals to control ants or other pests should never be used in the house, if possible. Your pup doesn't have to directly ingest these poisons to become ill; if your pit bull steps in the poison, he can experience toxic effects from licking these toxins off of his paws. Roach motels and other poisonous pest traps can also be attractive to dogs, so do not drop these behind couches or cabinets; if there's room for a roach motel, there's room for a determined APBT.

■ **Fabric:** Here's one you might not think about; some puppies have a habit of licking blankets, upholstery, rugs or carpets. Though this habit seems fairly innocuous, over time the fibers from the upholstery or carpet can accumulate in the dog's stomach and cause a blockage. If you see your dog licking these items, remove the item or prevent him from having contact with it.

■ **Prescriptions, painkillers, supplements and vitamins:** Keep all medications in a cabinet. Also, be very careful when taking your prescription medications, supplements or vitamins. How often have you dropped a pill? With an APBT, you can be sure that your puppy will

Did You Know?

Actor Humphrey Bogart and Lauren Bacall didn't have a complete home until they brought home a pit bull named Harvey!

give the item a taste test. Socks, coins, children's toys, game pieces, cat bell balls — you name it; if it's on the floor, it's worth a try. Make sure the floors in your home are picked up and free of clutter.

FAMILY INTRODUCTIONS

Everyone in the house will be excited about the puppy's homecoming and will want to pet and play with him, but it is best to make the introduction low-key so as not to overwhelm the puppy. He will already be apprehensive. It is the first time he has been separated from his mother, littermates and the breeder, and the ride to your home is likely to be the first time he has been in a car. The last thing you want to do is smother your APBT, as this will only frighten him further. This is not to say that human contact is not extremely necessary at this stage because this is the time when a connection between the pup and his human family is formed. Gentle petting and soothing words should help console your APBT, as well as just putting him down and letting him explore on his own (under your watchful eye, of course).

Your dog may approach the family members or may busy himself with exploring for a while. Gradually, each person should spend some time with the pup, one at a time, crouching down to get as close to the APBT's level as possible and letting him sniff their hands before petting him gently. He definitely needs human attention and he needs to be touched; this is how to form an

be at your feet and will snarf up the pill before you can even start to say "No!" Dispense your own pills carefully and without your APBT present.

■ **Miscellaneous loose items:** If it's not bolted to the floor, your puppy is likely to

---

The first thing you should always do before your puppy comes home is to lie on the ground and look around. You want to be able to see everything your puppy is going to see. For the puppy, the world is one big chew toy.

— Cathleen Stamm, rescue volunteer in San Diego, Calif.

immediate bond. Just remember that the pup is experiencing a lot of things for the first time, at the same time. There are new people, noises, smells and things to investigate, so be gentle, be affectionate and be as comforting as possible.

PUP'S FIRST NIGHT HOME

You have traveled home with your new charge safely in his crate. He may have already been to the vet for a thorough check-up — he's been weighed, his papers examined, perhaps he's even been vaccinated and dewormed, as well. Your APBT has met and licked the whole family, including the excited children and the less-than-happy cat. He's explored his area, his new bed, the yard and anywhere else he's permitted. He's

SMART TIP!

9-1-1! If you don't know whether the plant or food or "stuff" your pit bull just ate is toxic to dogs, you can call the ASPCA's Animal Poison Control Center (888-426-4435). Be prepared to provide your dog's age and weight, his symptoms — if any — and how much of the plant, chemical or substance he ingested, as well as how long ago you think he came into contact with the substance. The ASPCA charges a consultation fee for this service.

Make your home as comfortable as possible for your pit bull.

Even older dogs need items and places to call their own. As your dog grows, buy him new toys and bedding as those items age.

eaten his first meal at home and relieved himself in the proper place. Your APBT has heard lots of new sounds, smelled new friends and seen more of the outside world than ever before.

This was just the first day! He's worn out and is ready for bed — or so you think! Remember, this is your puppy's first night to sleep alone. His mother and littermates are no longer at paw's length and he's scared, cold and lonely. Be reassuring to your new family member, but this is not the time to spoil your APBT and give in to his inevitable whining.

Puppies whine. They whine to let others know where they are and hopefully to get company out of it. Place your APBT puppy in his new bed or crate in his room and close the door. Mercifully, he may fall asleep without a peep. If the inevitable occurs, ignore the whining; he is fine. Do not give in and visit your pit bull puppy. Don't worry, he will fall asleep eventually.

Many breeders recommend placing a piece of bedding from his former home in his new bed so that he recognizes the scent of his littermates. Others advise placing a hot water bottle in his bed for warmth. The latter may be a good idea provided the pup doesn't attempt to suckle; he'll get good and wet and may not fall asleep so fast.

Your APBT's first night can be somewhat terrifying for him and his new family. Remember that you set the tone of nighttime at your house. Unless you want to play with your pup every night at 10 p.m., midnight and 2 a.m., don't initiate the habit. Your family will thank you, and so will your pup!

SHOPPING FOR AN APBT

It's fun shopping for a new puppy. From training to feeding and sleeping to playing, your new pit bull will need a few items to

NOTABLE & QUOTABLE

Playing with toys from puppyhood encourages good behavior and social skills throughout the dog's life. A happy, playful dog is a content and well-adjusted one. Also, because all puppies chew to soothe their gums and help loosen puppy teeth, dogs should always have easy access to several different toys.

— *dog trainer and author Harrison Forbes of Savannah, Tenn.*

make life comfy, easy and fun. Be prepared and visit your local pet-supply store before you bring home your new family member.

◆ **Collar and ID tag:** Accustom your dog to wearing a collar the first day you bring him home. Not only will a collar and ID tag help your pup in the event that he becomes lost, but collars are also an important training tool. If your pit bull gets into trouble, the collar will act as a handle, helping you divert him to a more appropriate behavior. Make sure the collar fits snugly enough so your pit

bull cannot wriggle out of it but is loose enough so it will not be uncomfortably tight around his neck. You should be able to fit a finger between the pup and the collar. Collars come in many styles, but for starting out, a simple buckle collar with an easy-release snap works great.

◆ **Leash:** For training or just for taking a stroll down the street, a leash is your pit bull's vehicle to explore the outside world. Like collars, leashes come in a variety of styles and materials. A 6-foot nylon leash is a popular choice because it is lightweight and durable. As your pup grows and gets used to walking on the leash, you may want to purchase a flexible leash. These leads allow you to extend the length to give the dog a broader area to explore or to shorten the length to keep the dog closer to you.

◆ **Bowls:** Your pit bull will need two bowls — one for water and one for food. You may want two sets of bowls, one for inside

A well-fitting collar and ID tag are must-have items for your dog. Make sure you purchase ones that are appropriately sized.

and one for outside, depending on where the dog will be fed and where he will be spending time. Bowls should be sturdy enough so that they don't tip over easily. (Most have reinforced bottoms that prevent tipping.) Bowls usually are made of metal, ceramic or plastic and should be easy to clean.

◆ **Crate:** A multipurpose crate serves as a bed, housetraining tool and travel carrier. It also is the ideal doggie den — a bedroom of

sorts — that your pit bull can retire to when he wants to rest or just needs a break. The crate should be large enough for your pit bull to stand in, turn around and lie down. You don't want any more room than this — especially if you're planning on using the crate to housetrain your dog — because he will eliminate in one corner and lie down in another. Get a crate that is big enough for your dog when he is an adult. Then, use dividers to limit the space for when he's a puppy.

◆ **Bed:** A plush doggie bed will make sleeping and resting more comfortable for your pit bull. Dog beds come in all shapes, sizes and colors, but your dog just needs one that is soft and large enough for him to stretch out on. Because puppies and rescue dogs often don't come housetrained, it's helpful to buy a bed that can be washed easily. If your pit bull will be sleeping in a crate, a nice crate pad and a small blanket that he can "burrow" in will help him feel more at home. Replace the blanket if it becomes ragged and starts to fall apart because your pit bull's nails could get caught in it.

◆ **Gate:** Similar to those used for toddlers, gates help keep your pit bull confined to one room or area when you can't supervise him. Gates also work to keep your dog out of areas you don't want him in. Gates are

Your pit bull puppy will look to you to be his caregiver, best friend and pack leader.

When you are unable to watch your pit bull puppy, put him in a crate or an exercise pen on an easily cleanable floor. If he does have an accident on carpeting, clean it completely and meticulously, so that it does not forever smell like his potty accident.

BEYOND THE BASICS

The items previously discussed are the bare necessities. You will find out what else you need as you go along — grooming supplies, flea/tick protection, etc. These things will vary depending on your situation, but it is important that you have everything you need to make your APBT comfortable in his new home.

available in many styles. For pit bulls, make sure the one you choose has openings small enough so your puppy can't squeeze through the bars or any openings.

◆ **Toys:** Keep your dog occupied and entertained by providing him with an array of fun toys. Teething puppies like to chew — in fact, chewing is a physical need for pups as they are teething — and everything from your shoes to the leather couch to the fancy rug are fair game. Divert your pit bull's chewing instincts with durable toys like bones made of nylon or hard rubber.

Other fun toys include rope toys, treat-dispensing toys and balls. Make sure the toys and bones don't have small parts that could break off and be swallowed, causing your dog to choke. Stuffed toys can become destuffed and an overly excited pit bull puppy may ingest the stuffing or the squeaker. Check your APBT's toys regularly and replace them if they become frayed or show signs of wear.

◆ **Cleaning supplies:** Until your pit bull pup is housetrained, you will be doing a lot of cleaning. Accidents will occur, which is acceptable in the beginning because the puppy doesn't know any better. All you can do is be prepared to clean up any accidents. Old rags, towels, newspapers and a stain-and-odor remover are good to have on hand.

Pit bulls thrive on human interaction. Don't just give your dog a toy and then leave – stay and play with him for a while.

Some ordinary household items make great toys for your pit bull — as long you make them safe. You will find a list of homemade toys at **DogChannel.com/Club-APBT** — click "Downloads."

HOUSETRAINING

Unexciting as it may be, the housetraining part of puppy rearing greatly affects the budding relationship between a smart owner and his puppy — particularly when it becomes an area of ongoing contention. Fortunately, armed with suitable knowledge, patience and common sense, you'll find housetraining progresses at a relatively smooth rate. That leaves more time for the important things, like cuddling your adorable puppy, showing him off and laughing at his numerous antics.

The answer to successful housetraining is total supervision and management — crates, tethers, exercise pens and leashes — until you know your dog has developed substrate preferences for outside surfaces (grass, gravel, concrete) instead of carpet, tile or hardwood, and knows that pottying happens outside.

IN THE BEGINNING

For the first two to three weeks of a puppy's life, his mother helps the pup to eliminate. The mother also keeps the whelping box or, "nest area," clean. When pups begin to walk around and eat on their own, they choose where they eliminate. You can

> **it's a Fact**
>
> **Ongoing housetraining difficulties may indicate your puppy has a health problem,** warranting a veterinary checkup. A urinary infection, parasites, a virus, and other nasty issues greatly affect your puppy's ability to hold pee or poop.

train your puppy to relieve himself wherever you choose, but this must be somewhere suitable. You should bear in mind from the outset that when your puppy is old enough to go out in public places, any canine deposits must be removed at once. You will always have to carry with you a small plastic bag or "poop scoop."

Outdoor training includes such surfaces as grass, soil and concrete. Indoor training usually means training your dog on newspaper. When deciding on the surface and location that you will want your APBT to use, be sure it is going to be permanent. Training your dog on grass and then changing two months later is extremely difficult for dog and owner.

Next, choose the cue you will use each and every time you want your puppy to potty. "Let's go," "hurry up" and "potty" are examples of cues commonly used by smart dog owners.

Get in the habit of giving your puppy the chosen relief cue before you take him out. That way, when he becomes an adult, you will be able to determine if he wants to go out when you ask him. A confirmation will be signs of interest, such as wagging his tail, watching you intently or going to the door.

Did You Know?

Cleaning accidents properly with an enzyme solution will dramatically reduce the time it takes to house-train your dog because he won't be drawn back to the same areas.

LET'S START WITH THE CRATE

Clean animals by nature, dogs keenly dislike soiling where they sleep and eat. This fact makes a crate a useful tool for housetraining. When purchasing a crate, consider that one correctly sized will allow adequate room for an adult dog to stand full-height, lie on his side without scrunching and turn around easily. If debating plastic versus wire crates, short-haired breeds sometimes prefer the warmer, draft-blocking quality of plastic, while furry dogs often like the cooling airflow of a wire crate.

Some crates come equipped with a movable wall that reduces the interior size to provide enough space for your puppy to stand, turn and lie down, while not allowing room to soil one end and sleep in the other. The problem is if your puppy potties in the crate anyway, the divider forces him to lie in his own excrement.

This can work against you by desensitizing your puppy against his normal, instinctive revulsion to resting where he has eliminated. If scheduling permits you or a responsible family member to clean the crate soon after it's soiled, then you can continue to cratetrain because limiting crate size does encourage your puppy to hold it. Otherwise, give him enough room to move away from an unclean area until he's better able to control his elimination.

Needless to say, not every puppy adheres to this guideline. If your puppy moves along at a faster pace, thank your lucky stars. Should he progress slower, accept it and remind yourself that he'll improve. Be aware that pups frequently hold it longer at night than during the day. Just because your puppy sleeps for six or more hours through the night, it does not mean he can hold it that long during the more active daytime hours.

Housetraining a rescued adult pit bull might take some extra time and patience.

One last bit of advice on the crate: Place it in the corner of a normally trafficked room, such as the family room or kitchen. Social and curious by nature, dogs like to feel included in family happenings. Creating a quiet retreat by putting the crate in an unused area may seem like a good idea, but results in your puppy feeling insecure and isolated. Watching his people pop in and out of the crate room reassures your puppy that he's not forgotten.

PUPPY'S NEEDS

Your puppy needs to relieve himself after play periods, after each meal, after he has been sleeping, and any time he indicates that he is looking for a place to urinate or defecate.

The urinary and intestinal tract muscles of very young puppies are not fully developed. Therefore, like human babies, puppies need to relieve themselves frequently. Take your puppy out often — every hour for an 8-week-old, for example — and always immediately after sleeping and eating. The older the puppy, the less often he will need to relieve himself. Finally, as a mature, healthy adult, he will require only three to five relief trips per day.

HOUSING HELPS

Because the types of housing and control you provide for your APBT puppy have a direct relationship on the success of house-training, you must consider the various aspects of both before beginning training. Taking a new puppy home and turning him

Be consistent in your potty rituals. Don't play with your dog until after he potties.

loose in your house can be compared to turning a child loose in a sports arena and telling the child that the place is all his! The sheer enormity of the place would be too much for him to handle. Instead, offer the puppy clearly defined areas where he can play, sleep, eat and live. A room of the house where the family gathers is the most obvious choice. Puppies are social animals and need to feel like they are a part of the pack right from the start. Hearing your voice, watching you while you are doing things and smelling you nearby are all positive reinforcers that he is now a member of your pack. Usually a

NOTABLE & QUOTABLE

Reward your pup with a high-value treat immediately after he potties to reinforce going in the proper location, then play for a short time afterward. This teaches that good things happen after pottying outside! — Victoria Schade a certified pet dog trainer from Annandale, Va.

If you acquire your puppy at 8 weeks of age, expect to take her out at least six to eight times a day. By the time she's about 6 months old, potty trips will be down to three or four times a day. A rule of thumb is to take your puppy out in hourly intervals equal to her age in months.

Chaining a dog outside is no type of life. Housetrain your pit bull and let him live a civilized life inside with you.

family room, the kitchen or a nearby adjoining breakfast area is ideal for providing safety and security for puppy and owner.

Within that room, there should be a smaller area that your APBT puppy can call his own. An alcove, a wire or fiberglass dog crate, or a fenced (not boarded!) corner from which he can view the activities of his new family will be fine. The size of the area or crate is the key factor here. The area must be large enough for the puppy to lie down and stretch out his body, yet small enough so that he cannot relieve himself at one end and sleep at the other without coming into contact with his droppings before he is fully trained to relieve himself outside.

Dogs are, by nature, clean animals and will not remain close to their relief areas unless forced to do so. In those cases, they then become dirty dogs and usually remain that way for life.

The designated area should be lined with clean bedding and a toy. Water must always be available, in a no-spill container, once the dog is reliably housetrained.

IN CONTROL

By control, we mean helping your pit bull puppy to create a lifestyle pattern that will be compatible to that of his human pack (that's you!). Just as we guide children to learn our way of life, we must show our pup when it is time to play, eat, sleep, exercise and entertain himself.

Your puppy should always sleep in his crate. He should also learn that, during times of household confusion and excessive human activity, such as at breakfast when family members are preparing for the day, he can play by himself in relative safety and comfort in his designated area. Each time you leave your APBT alone, he should understand exactly where he is to stay.

Other times of excitement, such as parties, can be fun for your pit bull puppy, provided that he can view the activities from the security of his designated area. This way, your dog is not underfoot and he is not being fed all sorts of tidbits that will probably cause him stomach distress, yet he still feels a part of the fun.

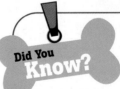

Did You Know? **White vinegar is a good odor remover** if you don't have any professional cleaners on hand. Use one-quarter cup to one quart of water.

SMART TIP!

When proximity prevents you from going home at lunch or during periods when overtime crops up, make alternative arrangements for getting your puppy out. Hire a pet sitting or walking service, or enlist the aid of an obliging neighbor.

Do not scold your pit bull puppy for mistakes. Instead, praise him lavishly when he does something correctly.

SCHEDULE A SOLUTION

A puppy should be taken to his relief area each time he is released from his designated area, after meals, after play sessions and when he first awakens in the morning (at age 8 weeks, this can mean 5 a.m.!). The puppy will indicate that he's ready "to go" by circling or sniffing busily; do not misinterpret these signs. For a puppy younger than 10 weeks of age, a routine of taking him out every hour is necessary. As the puppy grows older, he will be able to wait for longer periods of time without having to eliminate.

Keep trips to your puppy's relief area short. Stay no more than five or six minutes, then return to the house. If he goes during that time, praise him lavishly and take him indoors immediately. If he does not, but he has an accident when you go back indoors, pick him up immediately, say "No! No!" and return to his relief area. Wait a few minutes, then return to the house again. Never spank your puppy or rub his face in urine or excrement when he has had an accident.

Once indoors, put your puppy in his crate until you have had time to clean up his accident. Then release him to the family area and watch him more closely than before. Chances are, his accident was a result of your not picking up his potty signals or waiting too long before offering him the opportunity to relieve himself. Never hold a grudge against your puppy for accidents.

Let the puppy learn that going outdoors means it is time to relieve himself, not to play. Once trained, he will be able to play indoors and out and differentiate between the times for play versus the times for relief.

10 HOUSETRAINING HOW-TOs

1. Decide where you want your pit bull to eliminate. Take her there every time until she gets the idea. Pick a spot that's easy to access. Remember, puppies have very little time between "gotta go" and "oops."

2. Teach an elimination cue, such as "go potty" or "get busy." Say this every time you take your pit bull to eliminate. Don't keep chanting the cue, just say it once or twice, then keep quiet so you won't distract your dog.

3. Praise calmly when your dog eliminates, but stand there a little longer in case there's more.

4. Keep potty outings for potty only. Take your dog to the designated spot, tell her "go potty" and just stand there. If she needs to eliminate, she will do so within five minutes.

5. Don't punish for potty accidents; punishment can hinder progress. If you catch your pit bull in the act indoors, verbally interrupt but don't scold. Gently carry or lead your pup to the approved spot, let her finish, then praise.

6. If it's too late to interrupt an accident, scoop the poop or blot up the urine afterward with a paper towel. Immediately take your pit bull and her deposit (gently!) to the potty area. Place the poop or trace of urine on the ground and praise the pup. If she sniffs at her waste, praise more. Let your pit bull know you're pleased when her waste is in the proper area.

7. Keep track of when and where your APBT eliminates. That will help you anticipate potty times. Regular meals mean regular elimination, so feed your dog scheduled, measured meals instead of free-feeding (leaving food available at all times).

8. Hang a bell on a sturdy cord from the doorknob. Before you open the door to take your pit bull out for potty, shake the string and ring the bell. Most dogs soon realize the connection between the bell ringing and the door opening, then they'll try it out for themselves. Listen for that bell!

9. Dogs naturally return to where they've previously eliminated, so thoroughly clean up all accidents. Household cleaners will usually do the job, but special enzyme solutions may work better.

10. If the ground is littered with too much waste, your pit bull may seek a cleaner place to eliminate. Scoop the potty area daily, leaving just one "reminder."

Help him develop regular hours for naps, being alone, playing by himself and simply resting, all in his crate. Encourage him to entertain himself while you are busy. Let him learn that having you nearby is comforting, but it is not your main purpose in life to provide him with undivided attention.

Each time you put your pit bull puppy in his own area, use the same cue, whatever suits you best. Soon he will run to his crate or spe-

cial area when he hears you say those special words.

Remember that one of the primary ingredients in housetraining your puppy is control. Regardless of your lifestyle, there will always be occasions when you will need to have a place where your dog can stay and be happy and safe. Cratetraining is the answer for now and in the future.

A few key elements are really all you need for a successful housetraining method — consistency, frequency, praise, control and supervision. By following these procedures with a normal, healthy puppy, you and your dog will soon be past the stage of accidents and ready to move on to a full and rewarding life together.

JOIN OUR ONLINE
Club APBT®

Having housetraining problems with your pit bull? Ask other American Pit Bull Terrier owners for advice and tips. Log onto **DogChannel.com/Club-APBT** and click on "Community."

EVERYDAY CARE

Your selection of a veterinarian should be based on personal recommendation considering the doctor's skills with dogs, and, if possible, specifically pit bulls. If the vet is based nearby, it will be helpful in the case of an emergency or need for multiple treatments.

FIRST STEP: SELECT THE RIGHT VET

All licensed veterinarians are capable of dealing with routine medical issues such as infections and injuries, as well as the promotion of health (for example, by vaccinations). If the problem affecting your APBT is more complex, your vet will refer you to someone with more detailed knowledge of what is wrong. This usually will be a specialist like a veterinary dermatologist, veterinary ophthalmologist or whichever specialty service you require.

Veterinary procedures are very costly and, as the treatments available improve, they are only going to become more expensive. It is quite acceptable to discuss matters of cost with your vet. If there is more than one treatment option, cost may be a factor in deciding which route to take.

Smart owners will look for a veterinarian before they actually need one. Newbie pet owners should start looking for a veterinarian a month or two before they bring home a new APBT puppy. That will give them time to meet candidate veterinarians, check out the condition of the clinic, meet the staff and see who they feel most comfortable with. If you already have an APBT puppy, look sooner rather than later, preferably not in the midst of a veterinary health crisis.

Second, define the criteria that are important to you. Points to consider or investigate:

Convenience: Proximity to your home, extended hours or drop-off services are helpful for people who work regular business hours, have a busy schedule or do not want to drive far. If you have mobility issues, finding a vet who makes house calls or a service that provides pet transport might be particularly important.

Size: A one-person practice ensures that you will always deal with the same vet during each and every visit. "That person can really get to know both you and your dog," says Bernadine Cruz, D.V.M., of Laguna Hills Animal Hospital in Laguna Hills, Calif. The downside, though, is that the sole practitioner does not have the immediate input of another vet, and if your vet becomes ill or takes time off, you are out of luck.

The multiple-doctor practice offers consistency if your pit bull needs to come in unexpectedly on a day when your veterinarian isn't there. Additionally, your vet can quickly consult with his colleagues within the clinic if he's unsure about a diagnosis or a treatment.

If you find a veterinarian within that practice who you really like, you can make your appointments with that individual, establishing the same kind of bond that you would with a solo practitioner.

Appointment Policies: Some vet practices are strictly by-appointment only, which could minimize your wait time. However, if a sudden problem arises with your APBT and the veterinarians are booked, they might not be able to squeeze your dog in that day. Some clinics are walk-in only, great for crisis or impromptu visits, but without scheduling may involve longer waits to see the next available veterinarian — whoever is open, not someone in particular. Some practices offer the best of both worlds by maintaining an appointment schedule but also keep slots open throughout the day for walk-ins.

Basic vs. State-of-the-Art vs. Full Service: A practice with high-tech equipment offers greater diagnostic capabilities and treatment options, important for tricky or difficult cases. However, the cost of pricey equipment is passed along to the client, so you could pay more for routine procedures—the bulk of most pets' appointments. Some practices offer boarding, grooming, training classes and other services on the premises — conveniences some pet owners appreciate.

Fees and Payment Polices: How much does a routine office call cost? If there is a significant price difference, ask why. If you intend to carry health insurance on your pit bull or want to pay by credit card, make sure the candidate clinic accepts those payment options.

FIRST VET VISIT

It is much easier, less costly and more effective to practice preventive medicine than to fight bouts of illness and disease. Properly bred puppies of all breeds come from parents who were selected based upon their genetic disease profile. The puppies' mother should have been vaccinated, free of all internal and external parasites, and

Obesity is linked to an earlier onset of age-related health problems. Keep weight in check by providing sufficient exercise and play, and by feeding proper serving sizes. Calorie requirements decline as your puppy reaches adulthood and can drop 25 to 30 percent within a couple of months after your dog has been spayed or neutered; you'll probably need to reduce serving portions and switch to a less calorie-dense diet.

properly nourished. For these reasons, a visit to the veterinarian who cared for the dam (mother) is recommended if at all possible. The dam passes disease resistance to her puppies, which should last from eight to 10

Don't wait until an illness or injury comes up. Schedule regular vet visits to be sure your pit bull is in tip-top form.

weeks. Unfortunately, she can also pass on parasites and infection. This is why knowledge about her health is useful in learning more about the health of the puppies.

Now that you have your APBT puppy home safe and sound, it's time to arrange your pup's first trip to the veterinarian. Perhaps the breeder can recommend someone in the area who specializes in pit bulls, or maybe you know other APBT owners who can suggest a good vet. Either way, you should make an appointment within a couple of days of bringing home your puppy. If possible, see if you can stop by for this first vet appointment before going home.

The pup's first vet visit will consist of an overall examination to make sure that he does not have any problems that are not apparent to you. The veterinarian also will set up a schedule for the pup's vaccinations; the breeder will inform you of which ones the dog has already received and the vet can continue from there.

Your pit bull also will have his teeth examined and have his skeletal conformation and general health checked prior to certification by the veterinarian. Puppies in certain breeds have problems with their kneecaps, cataracts and other eye problems, heart murmurs and undescended testicles. They may also have personality problems; your veterinarian might even have training in temperament evaluation.

VACCINATION SCHEDULING

Most vaccinations are given by injection and should only be given by a veterinarian. Both you and the vet should keep a record of the date of the injection, the identification of the vaccine and the amount given. Some vets give a first vaccination at 8 weeks of age, but most dog breeders prefer the course not to commence until about 10 weeks

because of interaction with the antibodies produced by the mother. The vaccination scheduling is usually based on a 15-day cycle. You must take your vet's advice as to when to vaccinate, as this may differ according to the vaccine used.

The usual vaccines contain immunizing doses of several different viruses such as distemper, parvovirus, parainfluenza and hepatitis. There are other vaccines available when the puppy is at risk; you should rely on your vet's advice. This is especially true for the booster immunizations. Most vaccination

Set up a vet visit before you even bring your new dog home, so you can meet and interview the veterinarian staff.

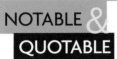
NOTABLE & QUOTABLE

*You need to exercise your dog. You need to keep your
APBT socialized, and you need to give him leadership
and direction. You need to not spoil him, but to teach him
to learn things.* — *Rande Levine, Karma Rescue president from Los Angeles, Calif.*

During your puppy's first few weeks at home, take him to the vet just to meet the staff and so he gets comfortable with the office. Call ahead, though, to make sure it is safe, as puppies are more susceptible to infectious disease.

programs require a booster when the puppy is a year old and once a year thereafter. In some cases, circumstances may require more frequent immunizations.

Kennel cough, more formally known as *tracheobronchitis*, is immunized with a vaccine that is sprayed into the dog's nostrils. Kennel cough is usually included in routine vaccinations, but it's usually not as effective as vaccines for other diseases.

Your veterinarian probably will recommend that your APBT puppy be fully vaccinated before you take him on outings. There are airborne diseases, parasite eggs in the grass and unexpected visits from other dogs that might be dangerous to your puppy's health. Other dogs are the most harmful reser-

voir of pathogenic organisms, as everything they have can be transmitted to your puppy.

6 Months to 1 Year of Age: Unless you intend to breed or show your dog, neutering/spaying your puppy at 6 months of age is recommended. Discuss this with your veterinarian. Neutering/spaying has proven to be beneficial to male and female puppies, respectively. Besides eliminating the possibility of pregnancy, it inhibits (but does not prevent) breast cancer in females and prostate cancer in male dogs.

Your veterinarian should provide your APBT puppy with a thorough dental evaluation at 6 months, ascertaining whether all his permanent teeth have erupted properly. A home dental care regimen should be initi-

NOTABLE & QUOTABLE

Pits have so many qualities not present in other breeds, and the love and loyalty they offer to their people is unexplainable. They are abused, neglected and tortured more frequently and in more horrific ways than any other breed; yet, they possess more affection and loyalty than any human could even imagine.

— *Amanda Conrad, president of Pit Prints Pit Bull Rescue/Rehabilitation in Canton, Ga.*

When selecting a veterinarian, make sure he or she is familiar with American Pit Bull Terriers.

Pit Bulls Rock

We Love Pit Bulls

ated at 6 months, including brushing weekly and providing good dental devices (such as nylon bones). Regular dental care promotes healthy teeth, fresh breath and a longer life.

Dogs Older Than 1 Year: Continue to visit the veterinarian at least once a year. There is no such disease as "old age," but bodily functions do change as your dog gets older. The eyes and ears are no longer as efficient; liver, kidney and intestinal functions often decline; and proper dietary changes, recommended by your veterinarian, can make life more pleasant for your aging APBT and you.

EVERYDAY HAPPENINGS

Keeping your pit bull healthy is a matter of keen observation and quick action when necessary. Knowing what's normal for your dog will help you recognize signs of trouble before they blossom into a full-blown emergency situation.

Even if the problem is minor, such as a cut or scrape, you'll want to care for it immediately to prevent infection, as well as to ensure that your dog doesn't make it worse by chewing or scratching at it. Here's what to do for common, minor injuries or illnesses and how to recognize and deal with emergencies.

Vets aren't just for vaccinating puppies; adult dogs need regular checkups, too.

Just like with infants, puppies need a series of vaccinations to ensure that they stay healthy during their first year of life. Download a vaccination chart from **DogChannel.com/Club-APBT** that you can fill out for your American Pit Bull Terrier.

Cuts and Scrapes: For a cut or scrape that's half an inch or smaller, clean the wound with saline solution or warm water and use tweezers to remove any splinters or other debris. Apply antibiotic ointment. No bandage is necessary unless the wound is on a paw, which can pick up dirt when your dog walks on it. Deep cuts with lots of bleeding or those caused by glass or some other object should be treated by your veterinarian.

Cold Symptoms: Dogs don't actually get colds, but they can get illnesses that have similar symptoms, such as coughing, a runny nose or sneezing. Dogs cough for any number of reasons, from respiratory infections to inhaled irritants to congestive heart failure. Take your APBT to the veterinarian for prolonged coughing or coughing accompanied by labored breathing, runny eyes or nose or bloody phlegm.

A runny nose that continues for more than several hours requires veterinary attention, as well. If your American Pit Bull Terrier sneezes, he may have some mild nasal irritation that will go away on its own, but frequent sneezing, especially if it's accompanied by a runny nose, may indicate anything from allergies to an infection to something stuck in the nose.

Vomiting and Diarrhea: Sometimes dogs suffer minor gastric upsets when they eat a new type of food, eat too much, eat the contents of the trash can or become excited or anxious. Give your pit bull's stomach a rest by withholding food for 12 hours, and then feeding him a bland diet such as baby food or rice and chicken, gradually returning your APBT to his normal food. Projectile vomiting, or vomiting or diarrhea that continues for more than 48 hours, is another matter. If this happens, take your APBT to the veterinarian.

MORE HEALTH HINTS

An APBT's anal glands can cause problems if not evacuated periodically. In the wild, anal glands are cleared regularly to set the dog's mark, but in domestic dogs this function is no longer necessary; thus, their contents can build up and clog, causing discomfort. Signs that the anal glands on either side of the anus need emptying are if a APBT drags his rear end along the ground or keeps turning around to attend to the uncomfortable patch.

While care must be taken not to cause injury, anal glands can be evacuated by pressing gently on either side of the anal opening and by using a piece of cotton or a tissue to collect the foul-smelling matter. If anal glands are allowed to become impacted, abscesses can form, causing pain and the need for veterinary attention.

APBTs can get into all sorts of mischief, so it's not uncommon for them to inadvertently swallow something poisonous in the course of their investigations. Obviously, an urgent visit to your vet is required under such circumstances, but if possible, when you telephone him or her, you should advise which poisonous substance has been ingested, as different treatments are needed. Should it be necessary to cause your dog to vomit (which is not always the case with poisoning), a small lump of baking soda, given orally, will have an immediate effect. Alternatively, a teaspoon of salt or mustard, dissolved in water, will have a similar effect but may be more difficult to administer and not as quick in its action.

APBT puppies often have painful fits while they are teething. These are not usually serious and are fleetingly brief, caused only by the pain of teething. Of course you must be certain that the cause is not more serious, but giving a puppy something hard to chew on will usually be enough to solve this temporary problem.

No matter how careful you are with your precious pit bull, sometimes unexpected injuries happen. Be prepared for any emergency by creating a canine first-aid kit. Find out what essentials you need on **DogChannel.com/Club-APBT.** Click on "Downloads."

JOIN OUR
ONLINE
Club
APBT®

OF HEALTH

Strong and vigorous, muscular and agile, American Pit Bull Terriers are generally hardy and healthy dogs. Just as their athleticism, build and temperament result from generations of selective breeding, so, too, does much of the pit bull's overall health depend on careful and deliberate breeding decisions.

But sometimes nature has rude surprises. As with all mammals — purebred and mixed pit bulls, humans and animals — APBTs' genetic makeup includes defective genes that may cause genetic or hereditary disease. That's a fact of nature no creature escapes. And just as certain segments of the human population may be more susceptible to genetic diseases than others, certain pit bulls are more susceptible to particular genetic disorders.

Fortunately, responsible breeders can minimize and even eliminate the risk of dogs developing many of these hereditary illnesses. Thanks to the progressive efforts of many involved in the APBT fancy, today's breeders have screening tools as simple as blood tests or cheek swab samples that help indicate whether a particular breeding prospect or adoptive puppy carries defective genes for various genetic disorders. For diseases for which such screening tools are not yet available, carefully studying the health

Did You Know?

Dogs can get many diseases from ticks, including Lyme disease, Rocky Mountain spotted fever, tick bite paralysis and many others.

history of breeding prospects provides breeders with information to help them make decisions that promote sound health in the breed. In addition, APBT fanciers actively raise health research funds to help uncover more effective treatments and prevention of genetic disease.

CHRONIC HIP DYSPLASIA

Chronic hip dysplasia results in a loose hip joint and abnormal rubbing of the joint surfaces. The joint eventually becomes inflamed, causing chronic pain, and even, arthritis to develop.

Chronic hip dysplasia is the No. 1 genetic health problem in dogs, and the American Pit Bull Terrier is no exception. But APBTs are generally stoic dogs and may not express outward signs of hip dysplasia as readily as other dogs, points out Darryl Millis, D.V.M., Diplomate of the American College of Veterinary Surgeons.

Clinical signs include limping, difficulty getting up, stiffness, altered gait, struggling to go up stairs or get into a car, and reduced interest in play. Treatment depends upon severity and age of your dog at diagnosis.

Conservative treatments for mildly dysplastic dogs include:

● weight control. Shedding extra pounds is often enough to decrease or eliminate joint pain in dogs.

● joint prescription dog food formulated to help improve joint function. Choose a formula that contains omega-3 fatty acids for best results. "Some of these formulas also contain glucosamine and chondroitin, although the amounts may not be adequate," says Millis, who is also a professor of orthopedic surgery at the University of Tennessee, Knoxville. "These diets replace the need for separate supplementation with omega-3 fatty acids."

● glucosamine and/or chondroitin supplements to promote joint health (if not provided in adequate amounts in your dog's formula). "Studies in arthritic humans found that glucosamine/chondroitin supplements helped those with moderate to severe knee pain," Millis says. "We still need well-controlled, long-term studies in clinically affected animals, though."

● pain reducers (anti-inflammatories or pain medications prescribed under veterinary supervision). Some dogs respond better to one medication than another, so you may have to try a couple of different pain relievers before finding one that works best for your dog.

● regular exercise to maintain muscle tone, strength and range of motion in the joint. Regular, low-impact activity such as swimming or leash walks at a speed and distance that your dog can handle (not to the point of lameness or stiffness) are recommended.

Another good exercise is "dancing" the dog frontward. "Pick up the dog's forelimbs and walk him forward as you walk backward," Millis explains. "This strengthens the gluteal muscles and helps reduce arthritis pain. But

SMART TIP!

Many skin irritations can be prevented or reduced by employing a simple preventative regimen:

■ Keep your pit bull's skin clean and dry.
■ Shampoo your American Pit Bull Terrier regularly (particularly during the summer, which gives rise to allergies) with a hypoallergenic shampoo.
■ Rinse her coat thoroughly.
■ Practice good flea control.
■ Supplement her diet with fatty acids.

don't walk the dog backward, as this could cause hip pain because of the more extended position of the hip joint."

● TENS (transcutaneous electrical nerve stimulation), a device that uses electrical impulse to reduce pain. "We found positive response to that," Millis says. "Most treatments last 20 to 30 minutes."

● ESWT (extracorporeal shockwave therapy), a treatment that uses sound waves to induce pain relief. "We tested dogs that were pretty bad and found, in general, a single treatment lasted several months," Millis says. Studies elsewhere found that less severely affected dogs achieved pain relief for up to two years.

More severely affected dogs as well as young dogs may best be served by surgical resolutions. Surgical options include:

● JPS (juvenile pubic symphysidesis). If diagnosed before a puppy reaches 14 to 16 weeks of age, this simple, minimally invasive procedure can be performed, often in combination with an early spay or neuter. With this procedure, growing cartilage cells in the lower pelvis are cauterized to create a tighter hip joint. "Most puppies aren't symptomatic by that age," Millis notes, "but for high-risk APBTs or loose-hipped puppies, it may be beneficial to perform JPS prophylactically during a spay or neuter."

● TPO (triple pelvic osteotomy), whereby the pelvic bone is cut in three places and repositioned to better secure the hip femoral head. "TPO is best performed in growing dogs with minimal or no arthritic changes," Millis states. "It doesn't work as well after arthritic changes have occurred. That's a mistake some dog owners make: They adopt a wait-and-see attitude and in as little as two to four weeks lose their window of opportunity for that procedure."

● femoral head and neck incision. Best for dogs weighing less than 50 pounds, this technique removes the femoral head and neck, forming a false joint.

● hip replacement surgery. Although this is an expensive operation and the recovery period is lengthy, hip replacement surgery provides the dog with a more functional, albeit artificial hip. "Many dogs with a hip replacement have a profound improvement in the quality of their life," Millis says.

Prognosis varies, depending upon treatment options and the severity of the disease. Mildly affected dogs are often given conservative treatment for a long time. The outlook for hip repair and reconstruction generally ranges from good to excellent.

Although hip dysplasia is undoubtedly linked to a dog's genetic makeup, other factors including overfeeding and over- or under-supplementation of carbohydrates, calcium and phosphorous in growing dogs also contribute to chronic hip dysplasia. Talk with your veterinarian to find the appropriate diet formula for your puppy or young dog to reduce the risk.

LUXATED PATELLA

A slipped kneecap (patellar luxation) occurs when the patella (a flat, movable bone at the front of the knee) pops out of place. A common hereditary disorder, luxated patellas usually affect both knee joints and tend to afflict dogs 6 months or younger, although dogs can be older when the disorder is first noticed. Trauma to the knee can also force the patella out of place.

The rear lower leg seems to momentarily lock, causing a skipping or hopping gait. In mild cases, the patella drops back into place again, but in more serious cases, the luxation occurs more frequently for longer periods with the dog exhibiting lameness or discomfort.

Mild cases of occasional luxations without residual lameness don't need treatment, although monitoring and veterinary re-evaluation are important in case the luxation worsens. Otherwise, dogs with more frequent or extended luxations, or those exhibiting lameness or discomfort, should undergo surgical correction soon after diagnosis to avoid exacerbating joint damage and prevent permanent lameness.

When treated promptly, prognosis for a full recovery is usually good. Keep in mind that the more damage the patella joint undergoes, the more difficult and expensive it is to repair the abnormalities and to achieve complete surgical correction.

DEMODECTIC MANGE

"The most prevalent complaint concerning a genetic health issue in the American Pit Bull Terrier is demodectic mange," says Amy G. Burford of the American Dog Breeders Association Inc. Also known as "demodicosis" or simply as "mange," the condition is a common cause of hair loss in dogs.

Demodicosis is caused by an overgrowth of demodex mites, microscopic arachnids that normally live harmlessly and in low numbers on animal skin. There are two forms: localized, which tends to occur on puppies between 3 and 6 months of age, and generalized, which occurs primarily in adult dogs.

Causes aren't always understood or identified. "In young dogs, it is presumed that genetic factors may predispose dogs to get demodicosis," says Dr. Thierry Olivry, a Diplomate in the American and European Colleges of Veterinary Dermatology.

In senior dogs, there are four scenarios that have been associated with demodicosis: steroid administration, hypothyroidism, Cushing's disease and chemotherapy. "In some cases, we don't know the initiating cause," says Olivry, a professor of immuno-dermatology at the North Carolina State University College of Veterinary Medicine. In the vast majority of cases, demodicosis is not contagious to humans or other pets."

Localized demodicosis manifests as small patches of hair loss with redness and scaling, and is confined to the face, head and front legs, Olivry explains. Generalized demodicosis spreads across the body, growing into larger, coalescing patches. In about 10 percent of affected puppies, demodicosis becomes generalized. Diagnosis is made with a microscopic exam of skin scrapes or hair plucks.

An Amitraz (Mitaban) dip every other week is the only FDA-approved treatment, Olivry reports. (Amitraz is a topical antiparasitic agent.) Other proven, effective measures are either increased Amitraz dips or daily applications of either ivermectin or milbemycin (drugs commonly used in heartworm prevention).

"Generally, treatment is continued until the dog receives two negative skin scrapes, one month apart," he says.

Prognosis is generally good. "Localized juvenile demodicosis tends to get better faster than adult onset," Olivry says. "Generalized demodicosis can take 3 months or more for complete remission of signs and another 3 to 6 months until scrapes are negative." Be aware that relapses often occur after treatment is discontinued.

AIRBORNE ALLERGIES

Just as humans suffer from hay fever during the pollinating season, many dogs suffer from the same allergies. When the pollen count is high, your APBT might suffer, but don't expect him to sneeze or have a runny nose like a human. Dogs react to pollen

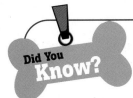

Did You Know? Across the globe, more than 800 species of ticks exist, and they aren't particular to where they dine. Mammals, birds and reptiles are all fair game.

allergies in the same way they react to fleas; they scratch and bite themselves. Dogs, like humans, can be tested for allergens. Discuss testing your dog for allergies with your vet.

AUTO-IMMUNE ILLNESS

An auto-immune illness is one in which the immune system overacts and does not recognize parts of the affected person. Instead, the immune system starts to react and turns against the body's cells as if they were foreign cells and therefore must be destroyed. An example is rheumatoid arthritis, which occurs when the body does not

recognize the joints, and this leads to a very painful and damaging reaction in the joints. This has nothing to do with age, so it can occur in puppies. The wear-and-tear arthritis in older people or dogs is called *osteoarthritis*.

Lupus is another auto-immune disease that affects dogs as well as people. It can take variable forms, affecting the kidneys, bones and the skin. It can be fatal, so it is treated with steroids, which can trigger very harsh side effects.

Steroids calm down the allergic reaction to the body's tissues, which helps the lupus, but it also calms down the body's reaction to actual foreign substances such as bacteria — making your dog vulnerable to other illnesses — and also thins the skin and bones.

FOOD ALLERGIES

Feeding your APBT properly is very important. An incorrect diet could affect your dog's health, behavior and nervous system, possibly making a normal dog aggressive. The result of a good or bad diet is most visible in a dog's skin and coat, but internal organs are affected, too.

Dogs are allergic to many foods that are popular and recommended by breeders and veterinarians. Changing the brand of food may not eliminate the problem if the ingredient to which your dog is allergic is contained in the new brand.

Recognizing a food allergy can be difficult. Humans often have rashes or swelling of the lips or eyes when they eat foods they are allergic to. Dogs do not usually develop rashes, but they react the same way they do to an airborne or bite allergy; they itch, scratch and bite. While pollen allergies and parasite bites are usually seasonal, food allergies are continual problems.

Diagnosis of a food allergy is based on a 2- to 4-week dietary trial with a home-cooked diet fed with the exclusion of all other foods. The diet should consist of boiled rice or potato with a source of protein that your APBT has never eaten before, such as fresh or frozen fish, lamb or even something as exotic as pheasant. Water has to be the only drink, and it is important that no other foods are fed during this trial. If your dog's condition improves, try the original diet again to see if the itching resumes. If it does, then your dog is allergic to his original diet. You must find a diet that does not distress your dog's skin. Start with a commercially available hypoallergenic diet or the homemade diet that you created for the allergy trial.

Food intolerance is the inability of the dog to completely digest certain foods. This occurs because the dog does not have the enzymes necessary to digest some foodstuffs. All puppies have the enzymes necessary to digest canine milk, but some dogs do not have the enzymes to digest cow milk, resulting in loose bowels, stomach pains and flatulence.

Dogs often do not have the enzymes to digest soy or other beans. The treatment is to exclude these foods from your APBT's diet.

PARASITE BITES

Insect bites itch, erupt and may even become infected. Dogs have the same reaction to fleas, ticks and mites. When an insect lands on you, you can whisk it away with your hand. Unfortunately, when a dog is bitten by a flea, tick or mite, he can only scratch or bite. By the time your APBT has been bitten, the parasite has done its damage. It may also have laid eggs, which will cause further problems. The itching from parasite bites is probably due to the saliva injected into the site when the parasite sucks the dog's blood.

EXTERNAL PARASITES

Fleas: Of all the problems to which dogs are prone, none is better known and more frustrating than fleas. Flea infestation is relatively simple to cure but difficult to prevent.

To control flea infestation, you have to understand the flea's life cycle. Fleas are often thought of as a summertime problem, but centrally heated homes have made fleas a year-round problem. The most effective method of treating fleas is a two-stage approach: Kill the adult fleas, then control the development of pre-adult fleas (*pupae*). Unfortunately, no single active ingredient is effective against all stages of the flea life cycle.

Controlling fleas should be a two-pronged attack. First, the environment needs to be treated; this includes carpets and furniture, especially your APBT's bedding and areas underneath furniture. The environment should be treated with a household spray

Brush your dog's teeth every day. Plaque colonizes on the tooth surface in as little as six to eight hours, and if not removed by brushing, forms calculus (tartar) within three to five days. Plaque and tartar cause gum disease, periodontal disease, loosening of the teeth and tooth loss. In bad cases of dental disease, bacteria from the mouth can get into the bloodstream, leading to kidney or heart problems — either of which are life-shortening problems.

containing an insect growth regulator and an insecticide to kill the adult fleas. Most insecticides are effective against eggs and larvae; they actually mimic the fleas' own hormones and stop the eggs and larvae from developing into adult fleas. There are currently no treatments available to attack the pupae stage of the life cycle, so the adult insecticide is used to kill the newly hatched adult fleas before they find a host. Most insecticides are active for many months, while adult insecticides are only active for a few days.

When treating with a household spray, vacuum before applying the product. This stimulates as many pupae as possible to hatch into adult fleas. The vacuum cleaner should also be treated with an insecticide to prevent the eggs and larvae that have been collected in the vacuum bag from hatching.

The second stage of treatment is to apply an adult insecticide to your American Pit Bull Terrier. Traditionally, this would be in the form of a flea collar or a spray, but more recent innovations include digestible insecticides that poison the fleas when they ingest the dog's blood. Alternatively, there are drops that, when placed on the back of the

In young puppies, roundworms cause bloated bellies, diarrhea and vomiting. They are transmitted from the mother (through blood or milk). Affected pups will not appear as animated as normal puppies. The worms appear spaghetti-like, measuring as long as 6 inches!

dog's neck, spread throughout the hair and skin to kill adult fleas.

Ticks: Though not as common as fleas, ticks are found in tropical and temperate climates. They don't bite like fleas; they harpoon. They dig their sharp *proboscis* (nose) into your APBT's skin and drink the blood, which is their only food and drink. Ticks are controlled the same way fleas are controlled.

The American dog tick, *Dermacentor variabilis*, may be the most common dog tick in many areas, especially those areas where the climate is hot and humid. Most dog ticks have life expectancies of a week to six months, depending on climactic conditions. They can neither jump nor fly, but they can crawl slowly and can range up to 16 feet to reach a sleeping or unsuspecting dog.

Mites: Just as fleas and ticks can be problematic for your dog, mites can also lead to an itch fit. Microscopic in size, mites are related to ticks and generally take up permanent residence on their host animal — in this case, your APBT! The term "mange" refers to any infestation caused by one of the mighty mites, of which there are six varieties that smart dog owners should know about.

Keeping your dog and his area clean is the best method to ward off pests such as fleas and mites.

* The *Cheyletiellosis* mite is the hook-mouthed culprit associated with "walking dandruff," a condition that affects dogs as well as cats and rabbits. If untreated, this mange can affect a whole kennel of dogs and can be spread to humans, as well.

* The *Sarcoptes* mite causes intense itching on the dog in the form of a condition known as scabies or sarcoptic mange. Scabies is highly contagious and can be passed to humans. Sometimes an allergic reaction to the mite worsens the severe itching associated with sarcoptic mange.

* Ear mites, *Otodectes cynotis*, lead to otodectic mange, which commonly affects the outer ear canal of the dog, though other areas can be affected as well. Your vet can prescribe a treatment to flush out the ears and kill any eggs in the ears. A month of treatment is necessary to cure mange.

* Two other mites, that are less common in dogs, include *Dermanyssus gallinae* (the "poultry" or "red mite") and *Eutrombicula alfreddugesi* (the North American mite associated with *trombiculidiasis* or chigger infestation). The types of mange caused by both of these mites must be treated by vets.

INTERNAL PARASITES

Most animals — fish, birds, and mammals, including dogs and humans — have worms and other parasites living inside their bodies. According to Dr. Herbert R. Axelrod, a fish pathologist, there are two kinds of parasites: dumb and smart. The smart parasites live in peaceful cooperation with their hosts (symbiosis), while the dumb parasites kill their hosts. Most worm infections are relatively easy to control. If they are not controlled, they weaken the host dog to the point that other medical problems occur, but they do not kill the host as dumb parasites would.

Roundworms: Roundworms that infect dogs live in the dog's intestines and shed eggs continually. It has been estimated that a dog produces about six or more ounces of feces every day. Each ounce averages hundreds of thousands of roundworm eggs. There are no known areas in which dogs roam that do not contain roundworm eggs. Because roundworms infect people too, it is wise to have your dog regularly tested.

Roundworm infection can kill puppies and cause severe problems in adult dogs, as the hatched larvae travel to the lungs and trachea through the bloodstream. Cleanliness is the best preventive for roundworms. Always pick up after your dog and dispose of feces in appropriate receptacles.

Hookworms: Hookworms are dangerous to humans as well as to dogs and cats, and can be the cause of severe anemia due to iron deficiency. The worm uses its teeth to attach itself to the dog's intestines and changes the site of its attachment about six times per day. Each time the worm repositions itself, the dog loses blood and can become anemic.

Symptoms of hookworm infection include dark stools, weight loss, general weakness, pale coloration and anemia as well as possible skin problems. Fortunately, hookworms are easily purged with a number of medications that have proven to be effective. Discuss these with your veterinarian. Most heartworm preventatives also include a hookworm insecticide.

Humans, can be infected by hookworms through exposure to contaminated feces. Because the worms cannot complete their life cycle in a human, the worms simply infest the skin and cause irritation. As a preventive, use disposable gloves or a "poop-scoop" to pick up your dog's droppings. In addition, be sure to prevent your dog (or neighborhood cats) from defecating in children's play areas.

Tapeworms: There are many species of tapeworm, all of which are carried by fleas! Fleas are so small that your APBT could pass them onto your hands, your plate or your food, making it possible for you to ingest a flea that is carrying tapeworm eggs. While tapeworm infection is not life-threatening in dogs (smart parasite!), it can be the cause of a very serious liver disease in humans.

Whipworms: In North America, whipworms are counted among the most common parasitic worms in dogs. Affected dogs may only experience upset tummies, colic and diarrhea. These worms, however, can live for months or years in the dog, beginning their larval stage in the small intestine, spending their adult stage in the large intestine and finally passing infective eggs through the dog's feces. The only way to detect whipworms is through a fecal examination, though this is not always foolproof. Treatment for whipworms is tricky, due to the worms' unusual life cycle, and often dogs are reinfected due to infective eggs on the

To control fleas, smart owners must treat their dog's environment as well as the dog himself

ground. Cleaning up droppings in your back-yard and in public places is absolutely essential for sanitation purposes and the health of your dog and others.

Threadworms: Though less common than roundworms, hookworms and previously mentioned parasites, thread-worms concern dog owners in the south-western United States and Gulf Coast area where it is hot and humid.

Living in the small intestine of the dog, this worm measures a mere two millimeters and is round in shape. Like the whipworm, the threadworm's life cycle is very complex, and the eggs and larvae are passed through the feces.

A deadly disease in humans, thread-worms readily infect people, mostly through the direct handling of feces. Threadworms are most often seen in young puppies. The most common symptoms include bloody diarrhea and pneumonia. Sick puppies must be isolated and treated immediately; vets recommend a follow-up treatment one month later.

Heartworms: Heartworms are thin, ex-tended worms up to 12 inches long, that live in a dog's heart and the major blood vessels surrounding it. Dogs may have up to 200 heartworms. Symptoms may be loss of energy, loss of appetite, coughing, the development of a pot belly and anemia.

Heartworms are transmitted by mosqui-toes, which drink the blood of infected dogs and take in larvae with the blood. The lar-vae, called microfilariae, develop within the body of the mosquito and are passed on to the next dog bitten after the larvae mature. It takes two to three weeks for the larvae to develop to the infective stage within the body of the mosquito. Dogs are usually treated at about six weeks of age and main-tained on a prophylactic dose given monthly.

Fleas used to be a only a summer concern, but with centrally heated homes, they now cause problems year round.

Blood testing for heartworms is not nec-essarily indicative of how seriously your dog is infected. Although this is a dangerous dis-ease, it is not easy for a dog to be infected. Discuss the various preventives with your vet, because there are many different types now available. Together you can decide on a safe course of prevention for your dog.

DIET

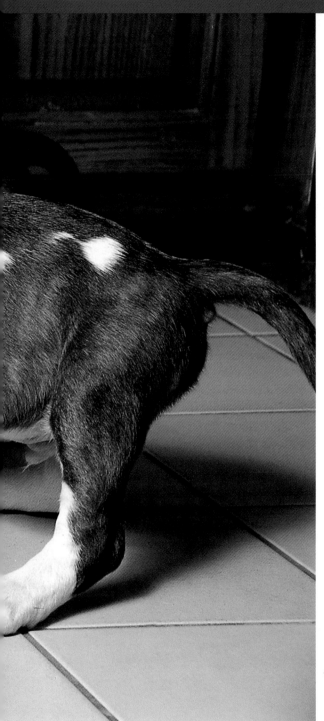

Y ou have probably heard it a thousand times: You are what you eat. Believe it or not, it is very true especially for dogs. Dogs are what you feed them because they have little choice in the matter. Even smart owners, who truly want to feed their dogs the best, often cannot do so because they don't know which foods are best for their dogs.

BASIC TYPES

Dog foods are produced in various types: dry, wet (canned), semimoist and frozen.

Dry food is useful for the cost-conscious owner because it tends to be less expensive than the others. This food also contains the least fat and the most preservatives. Dry food is bulky and takes longer to eat than other foods, so it's more filling.

Wet food — available in cans or foil pouches — is usually 60 to 70 percent water and is more expensive than dry food. A palatable source of concentrated nutrition, wet food also makes an excellent supplement for underweight dogs or those recovering from an illness. Some owners add a little wet food to dry food to increase its appeal, and dogs gobble up this mixture.

it's a **Fact**

Bones can cause gastrointestinal obstruction and perforation, and may be contaminated with salmonella or E. coli. Leave them in the trash and give your dog a nylon bone toy instead.

Semimoist food is flavorful but usually contains lots of sugar, which can lead to dental problems and obesity. It's not a good choice for your dog's main diet.

Likewise, **frozen food**, which is available in cooked and raw forms, is usually more expensive than wet food. The advantages of frozen food are similar to those of wet food.

The amount of food your APBT needs depends on a number of factors, such as age, activity level, food quality, reproductive status and size. What's the easiest way to figure it out? Start with the manufacturer's recommended amount, then adjust it according to your dog's response. For example, feed the recommended amount for a few weeks and if your APBT loses weight, increase the amount by 10 to 20 percent. If your dog gains weight, decrease the amount. It won't take long to determine the amount of food that keeps your little friend in optimal condition.

NUTRITION 101

All pit bulls (and every dog breed, for that matter) need proteins, carbohydrates, fats, vitamins and minerals for their optimal growth and health.

■ **Proteins** are used for growth and the repair of muscles, bones and other bodily tissues. They're also used for the production of antibodies, enzymes and hormones. All dogs need protein, but it's especially important for puppies because they grow so rapidly. Protein sources include various types of meat, meat meal, meat byproducts, eggs, dairy products and soybeans.

■ **Carbohydrates** are metabolized into glucose, the body's principle energy source. Carbohydrates are available as sugars, starches and fiber.

• Sugars (simple carbohydrates) are not suitable nutrient sources for dogs.

• Starch — a preferred type of carbohydrate in dog food — is found in a variety of plant products. Starches must be cooked in order to be digested.

• Fiber (cellulose) — also a preferred type of carbohydrates in dog food — isn't digestible, but it helps the digestive tract function properly.

■ **Fats** are also required for energy and play an important role in skin and coat health, hormone production, nervous system function and vitamin transport. Fat increases the palatability and the calorie count of puppy and dog food, which can contribute to serious health problems, such as obesity, for puppies or dogs who are allowed to overindulge. Some foods contain added amounts of omega fatty acids such as docosohexaenoic acid, a compound that

Believe it or not, during your pit bull's lifetime, you'll buy a few thousand pounds of dog food! Go to **DogChannel.com/Club-APBT** and download a chart that outlines the cost of dog food.

may enhance brain development and learning in pit bull puppies but is not considered an essential nutrient by the Association of American Feed Control Officials (www.aafco.org). Fats used in dog foods include tallow, lard, poultry fat, fish oil and vegetable oils.

■ **Vitamins** and **minerals** participate in muscle and nerve function, bone growth, healing, metabolism and fluid balance. Especially important for your puppy are calcium, phosphorus and vitamin D, which must

be supplied in the right balance to ensure proper development of bones and teeth.

Just as your dog needs proper nutrition from his food, water is an essential nutrient, as well. Water keeps a dog's body properly hydrated and promotes normal function of the body's systems. During housetraining, it is necessary to keep an eye on how much water your American Pit Bull Terrier is drinking, but once he is reliably trained, he should have access to clean, fresh water at all times, especially if you feed him dry food. Make sure that the dog's water bowl is clean, and change the water often.

CHECK OUT THE LABEL

To help you get a feel for what you are feeding your dog, start by taking a look at the nutrition labels. Look for the words "complete and balanced." This tells you that the food meets specific nutritional requirements set by the AAFCO for either adults ("maintenance") or puppies and pregnant/lactating females ("growth and reproduction"). The label must state the group for which it is intended. If you're feeding a puppy, choose a "growth and reproduction" food.

The label also includes a nutritional analysis, which lists minimum protein, minimum fat, maximum fiber and maximum moisture content, as well as other information. (You won't find carbohydrate content because it's everything that isn't protein, fat, fiber and moisture.)

The nutritional analysis refers to crude protein and crude fat — amounts that have been determined in the laboratory. This analysis is technically accurate, but it does not tell you anything about digestibility — how much of the particular nutrient your APBT can actually use. For information about digestibility, contact the manufacturer (check the label for a phone number and website).

Dogs of all ages love treats and table food, but these goodies can unbalance your pit bull's diet and lead to a weight problem if you don't choose and feed them wisely. Table food, whether fed as a treat or as part of a meal, shouldn't account for more than 10 percent of your dog's daily caloric intake. If you plan to give your APBT treats, be sure to include "treat calories" when calculating the daily food requirement, so you don't end up with a pudgy pup!

When shopping for packaged treats, look for ones that provide complete nutrition. They're basically dog food in a fun form. Choose crunchy goodies for chewing fun and dental health. Other ideas for tasty treats include:

✓ small chunks of cooked, lean meat
✓ dry dog food morsels
✓ cheese
✓ veggies (cooked, raw or frozen)
✓ breads, crackers or dry cereal
✓ unsalted, unbuttered, plain, popped popcorn

Some foods, however, can be dangerous or even deadly to a dog. The following can cause digestive upset (vomiting or diarrhea) or toxic reactions that could be fatal:

✗ **avocados:** can cause gastrointestinal irritation, with vomiting and diarrhea, if eaten in sufficient quantity

✗ **baby food:** may contain onion powder; does not provide balanced nutrition for a dog or pup

✗ **chocolate:** contains methylxanthines and theobromine, caffeine-like compounds that can cause vomiting, diarrhea, heart abnormalities, tremors, seizures and death. Darker chocolates contain higher levels of the toxic compounds.

✗ **eggs, raw:** whites contain an enzyme that prevents uptake of biotin, a B vitamin; may contain salmonella

✗ **garlic (and related foods):** can cause gastrointestinal irritation and anemia if eaten in sufficient quantity

✗ **grapes:** can cause kidney failure if eaten in sufficient quantity (the toxic dose varies from dog to dog)

✗ **macadamia nuts:** can cause vomiting, weakness, lack of coordination and other problems

✗ **meat, raw:** may contain harmful bacteria such as salmonella or E. coli

✗ **milk:** can cause diarrhea in some puppies

✗ **onions (and related foods):** can cause gastrointestinal irritation and anemia if eaten in sufficient quantity

✗ **raisins:** can cause kidney failure if eaten in sufficient quantity (the toxic dose varies from dog to dog)

✗ **yeast bread dough:** can rise in the gastrointestinal tract, causing obstruction; produces alcohol as it rises

Virtually all commercial puppy foods exceed the AAFCO's minimal requirements for protein and fat, the two nutrients most commonly evaluated when comparing foods. Protein levels in dry puppy foods usually range from about 26 to 30 percent; for canned foods, the values are about 9 to 13 percent. The fat content of dry puppy foods is about 20 percent or more; for canned foods, it's 8 percent or more. (Dry food values are larger than canned food values because dry food contains less water; the values are actually similar when compared on a dry matter basis.)

Finally, check the ingredients on the label, which lists the ingredients in descending order by weight. Manufacturers are allowed to list separately different forms of a single ingredient (e.g., ground corn and corn gluten meal). The food may contain things like meat byproducts, meat and bone meal, and animal fat, which probably won't appeal to you but are nutritious and safe for your dog. Higher quality foods usually have meat or meat products near the top of the ingredient list, but you don't need to worry about grain products as long as the label indicates that the food is nutritionally complete. Dogs are omnivores (not carnivores, as commonly believed), so all balanced dog foods contain animal and plant ingredients.

STAGES OF LIFE

When selecting your dog's diet, three stages of development must be considered: the puppy stage, the adult stage and the senior stage.

Puppy Diets: Pups instinctively want to nurse, and a normal puppy will exhibit this behavior from just a few moments following birth. Puppies should be allowed to nurse for about the first six weeks, although from the third or fourth week, the breeder will begin

Did You Know?

If you're feeding a puppy food that's complete and balanced, your pit bull youngster doesn't need any dietary supplements such as vitamins, minerals, or other types of food. Dietary supplementation could even harm your puppy by unbalancing his diet. If you have questions about supplementing your pit bull's diet, consult your veterinarian.

Feeding your dog is part of your daily routine. Take a break, and have some fun online and play "Feed the APBT," an exclusive game found only on **DogChannel.com/Club-APBT** — just click on "Games."

How can you tell if your pit bull is fit or fat? When you run your hands down your pal's sides from front to back, you should be able to easily feel his ribs. It's OK if you feel a little body fat (and, of course, a lot of hair), but you should not feel huge fat pads. You should also be able to feel your APBT's waist — an indentation behind the ribs.

to introduce small portions of suitable solid food. Most breeders like to introduce alternate milk and meat meals initially, building up to weaning time.

By the time puppies are 7 or a maximum of 8 weeks old, they should be fully weaned and fed solely a proprietary puppy food. Selection of the most suitable, good-quality diet at this time is essential, for a puppy's fastest growth rate is during the first year of his life. Seek advice about your dog's food from your veterinarian. The frequency of meals will be reduced over time, and when a young dog has reached about 10 to 12 months of age, he should be switched to an adult diet.

Puppy and junior diets can be balanced for the needs of your APBT so that, except in certain circumstances, additional vitamins, minerals and proteins will not be required.

How many times a day does your APBT need to eat? Puppies have small stomachs and high metabolic rates, so they need to eat several times a day in order to consume sufficient nutrients. If your puppy is younger than 3 months old, feed him four or five meals a day. When your little buddy is 3 to 5 months old, decrease the number of meals to three or four. At 6 months of age, most puppies can move to an adult schedule of two meals a day. If your APBT is prone to hypo-

glycemia (low blood sugar), a veterinarian may recommend more frequent meals.

Adult Diets: A dog is considered an adult when he has stopped growing. Rely on your veterinarian or dietary specialist to recommend an acceptable maintenance diet for your dog. Major dog food manufacturers specialize in this type of food, and smart owners must select the one best suited to their dogs' needs. Do not leave food out all day for "free-choice" feeding, as this freedom inevitably translates to inches around your dog's waist.

Senior Diets: As dogs get older, their metabolism changes. An older dog usually exercises less, moves more slowly and sleeps more. This change in lifestyle and physiological performance requires a change in diet. Because these changes take place slowly, they might not be recog-

A smart APBT owner reads all the nutrition labels on a package of dog food to ensure that his or her pit bull is getting all his vitamins and minerals.

nizable. These metabolic changes increase the tendency toward obesity, requiring an even more vigilant approach to feeding. Obesity in an older dog compounds the health problems that already accompany old age.

As your APBT gets older, few of his organs function up to par. The kidneys slow down, and the intestines become less efficient. These age-related factors are best handled with a change in diet and a change in feeding schedule to give smaller portions that are more easily digested.

There is no single best diet for every older dog. While many older dogs will do perfectly fine on light or senior diets, other dogs will do better on special premium diets such as

lamb and rice. A smart owner will be prudent and sensitive to his or her senior pit bull's diet, and this will help control other health complications that may arise with your old friend.

These delicious, dog-friendly recipes will have your furry friend smacking his lips and salivating for more. Just remember: Treats aren't meant to replace your dog's regular meals. Give your pit bull snacks sparingly and continue to feed him nutritious, well-balanced meals.

Cheddar Squares

⅓ cup all-natural applesauce
⅓ cup low-fat cheddar cheese, shredded
⅓ cup water
2 cups unbleached white flour

In a medium bowl, mix all wet ingredients. In a large bowl, mix all dry ingredients. Slowly add the wet ingredients to the dry mixture.

Mix well. Pour batter into a greased 13x9x2-inch pan. Bake at 375-degrees Fahrenheit for 25 to 30 minutes. Bars are done when a toothpick inserted in the center and removed comes out clean. Cool and cut into bars. Makes about 54, 1½-inch bars.

Peanut Butter Bites

3 tablespoons vegetable oil
¼ cup smooth peanut butter, no salt or sugar
¼ cup honey
1½ teaspoons baking powder
2 eggs
2 cups whole wheat flour

In a large bowl, mix all ingredients until dough is firm. If the dough is too sticky, mix in a small amount of flour. Knead dough on a lightly floured surface until firm. Roll out dough half an inch thick and cut with cookie cutters. Put cookies on a cookie sheet half an inch apart. Bake at 350-degrees Fahrenheit for 20 to 25 minutes. When done, cookies should be firm to the touch. Remove cookies from the oven, and leave cookies for one to two hours to harden. Makes about 40, 2-inch-long cookies.

When it comes to wash-and-wear breeds, the American Pit Bull Terrier tops the list as naturally fancy, sparkly and eye catching. Pit bulls don't require very much grooming, and the majority of their coat problems stem from a poor diet. Producing a healthy, glossy coat starts from the inside. Every dog's nutritional needs are slightly different, but coat dressing can never replace the natural shine that comes from good nutrition and good health.

No matter what the television commercial models with long, flowing tresses tell you, the ingredients you add externally to your dog's hair will not change a brittle, lifeless coat into a soft, healthy coat. The truth is that if you want your APBT to have a healthy coat, you need to take a close look at your dog's nutrition. Healthy hair and skin begins with good nutrition.

A good premium dog food is the best place to start growing a healthy coat. Your pit bull's diet is not the place to economize. Purchase the best food you can afford and resist the impulse to save money at your APBT's expense. Pit bulls' skin can be sensitive, so consult your veterinarian when choosing your dog's food. Once you've established a

Did You Know?

Nail clipping can be tricky, so many dog owners leave the task to the professionals. However, if you walk your dog on concrete, you may not have to worry about it. The concrete acts like a nail file and will probably keep the nails in check.

good nutritional basis, you can move on to improving the coat from the outside.

However, sometimes a dog, especially a playful APBT, gets dirty and needs to be gussied up. Here's how you do it.

GEAR UP

In order to keep a pit bull polished, a smart owner will need a few essential grooming tools:

- a pair of nail clippers
- styptic powder
- cotton balls
- ear powder or cleaner
- tearless pet shampoo
- a coat conditioner
- hydrogen peroxide or baby wipes
- a bristle brush or a slicker brush

LATHER, RINSE, REPEAT

American Pit Bull Terriers only need to be bathed once every eight weeks or so — or when they find a mud puddle to their liking. Bathing them too often removes natural oils from the coat. Some groomers prefer a high-quality medicated shampoo, which helps keep the skin in better condition, while many breeders avoid products containing tea tree oil.

Kim Swogger, a breeder in Wampum, Pa., sticks to natural shampoos. "This breed is known to have sensitive skin, and some pit bulls can be prone to skin problems. I like oatmeal shampoo. I would definitely stay away from generic, economy brands, but any shampoo can dry the skin if you use it too often."

A smart owner knows that keeping a pit bull beautiful starts with a healthy diet. Don't skimp; buy the best.

NOTABLE & QUOTABLE

After removing a tick, clean your dog's skin with hydro-gen peroxide. If Lyme disease is common where you live, have your veterinarian test the tick. Tick preventative medication will discourage ticks from attaching and kill any that do.

— *groomer Andrea Vilardi from West Paterson, N.J.*

American Pit Bull Terriers do not require much grooming to look fantastic. To give your already clean pit bull an extra glow, give him a rubdown with a chamois cloth or towel in addition to your already scheduled grooming routine.

Washing, rather than scrubbing, the coat minimizes the possibility of stripping coat oils or irritating sensitive skin. After completely wetting your dog, saturate a large bath sponge with shampoo and gently glide it over the entire coat. Do not pour the shampoo directly onto your dog. Work in the direction of the hair growth and do not rub or scrub. Rinse and repeat. A conditioning rinse is not recommended because it may soften the coat's natural texture. The final rinse should leave the coat squeaky clean. Make sure that no soap residue remains in the coat. If your dog's skin seems itchy or flaky the day after a bath, this is often due to inadequate rinsing.

The key to a successful bath is organization. Keep all your grooming tools in a basket so you can set up for the bath in only a moment. (This is handy when your zestful terrier finds something interesting in the yard to roll in and you must move quickly!)

Check the temperature of the water against the inside of your wrist or with your hand. Hold the hose close to your dog's body to eliminate excessive spray. If you don't have a hose attachment, use a plastic cup to scoop water and pour it over your dog.

Work from the highest point to the lowest on your pit bull with the water and shampoo; use your fingers to work the shampoo throughout the coat.

To keep water from getting into your dog's nose when you rinse this area, hold your hand as a barrier around the nose, and let the water flow from behind the ears toward your hand and sort of break against the hand. Rinse your dog with a gentle flow of water until his coat feels clean and the water runs clear.

When drying the coat, use a blotting technique, squeezing the hair instead of rubbing the towel back and forth. If you use a hair dryer, test the air flow against the inside of your wrist first, then hold it about 10 to 12 inches from the dog.

BRUSH THAT DOG!

Regular brushing, at least once a week, also contributes to healthy skin. Using a nat-

American Pit Bull Terriers require minimal grooming and only need to be bathed about once every eight weeks.

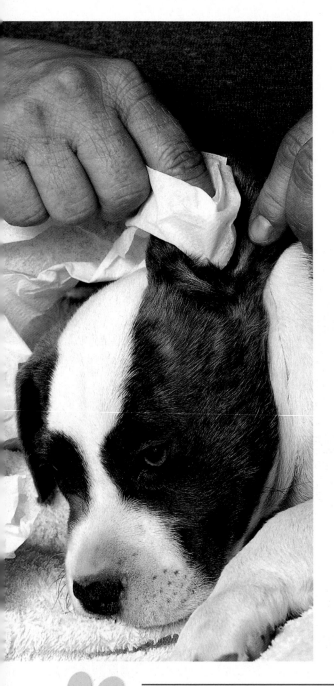

ural bristle brush or a slicker brush, brush the entire coat in firm, circular motions to loosen dead hair, stimulate the skin and increase the production of natural coat oils.

At the end of every coat growth cycle, hair dies and leaves the coat looking dull and lifeless until dead hair is shed and new growth emerges. Frequent brushing speeds up the process and stimulates regrowth from each hair follicle.

American Pit Bull Terriers shed minimally year-round and may experience pronounced seasonal shedding in the spring and fall. Seasonal shedding is more evident in climates with definite seasons because light has a big effect on coat growth. The seasonal coat change is more pronounced in outdoor dogs. Indoor dogs tend to have more year-round shedding. Regular dog brushes really aren't effective in either case because a pit bull's coat is so short.

NOW EAR THIS

Whether your dog has cropped or natural ears, they should be checked frequently and cleaned at least once a week. Cropped ears permit better air circulation, but there is a bigger risk of water or debris getting into the ear canal. Ear infections can become serious before you notice anything is wrong.

Symptoms of an ear problem include sensitivity to touch, heavy buildup of wax and debris, inflammation, odor, head shaking and scratching, or head tilting. Bacterial, fungal or yeast infections may also require specific veterinary treatment.

Moisture is a major source of infection;

JOIN OUR ONLINE Club APBT®

Every American Pit Bull Terrier should look dapper. What do you need to keep your dog looking his best? Go to Club APBT (**DogChannel.com/Club-APBT**) and download a checklist of essential grooming equipment you and your pit bull will need.

you can put cotton in your dog's ears before a bath to prevent water from getting into the ear canals. Ears should always be swabbed and dried carefully after swimming or bathing.

The canine ear canal makes an abrupt turn near the jaw, creating an ideal setting for infections. Ear-cleaning solution not only helps flush out debris, it also alters the ear's pH levels to discourage infection. Squirt enough ear-cleaning solution into your dog's ear to fill the canal and gently massage the

SMART TIP!

The family pet shouldn't be the center of a power struggle between children and parents. Divvy up grooming responsibilities early on, and make the issue non-negotiable. A clean pit bull is welcomed into the house with the family; a dirty one is banished to the backyard, doomed to be on the outside looking in. Even short-coated breeds such as APBTs need a regular grooming routine.

opening for a few seconds to loosen debris. Use a cotton ball to wipe away all visible moisture, earwax and dirt.

NAIL CLIPPING 4-1-1

Immediately after the bath is the best time to clip the nails because the water has softened the nails, and your APBT may be somewhat tired-out by the bath. Nail trimming is recommended every two weeks with nail clippers or a nail grinding tool. Short nails are crucial to maintaining the breed's normal foot shape. Long nails will permanently damage dog's feet, and the tight ligaments of round, arched feet will break down more quickly. If your dog's nails are clicking on the floor, this is a sign that they need to be trimmed.

When grinding, use a low-speed (5,000 to 10,000 rpm), cordless nail grinder fitted with a fine grade (100 grit) sandpaper cylinder. Stone cylinders are more prone to heat buildup and vibration. Hold your dog's paw firmly in one hand, spreading the toes slightly apart. Touch the spinning grinder wheel to the nail tip for one or two seconds without applying pressure. Repeat if necessary to remove only the nail tip protruding beyond the quick. Grinders have the added benefit of leaving nails smooth and free of sharp, jagged

edges produced by traditional nail clippers.

Your APBT should be accustomed to having his nails trimmed from an early age, because it will be part of your maintenance routine throughout his life. Not only does it look nicer, but long nails can also unintentionally scratch someone. Furthermore, a long nail has a better chance of ripping and bleeding, or causing the feet to spread.

Before you start cutting, make sure you can identify the "quick" (the vein in the center of each nail). It will bleed if accidentally cut, which will be quite painful for your dog as it contains nerve endings. Keep some type of clotting agent on hand, such as a styptic pencil or styptic powder (the type used for shaving). This will quickly stop the bleeding when applied to the end of the cut nail. Do not panic if this happens; just stop the bleeding and talk soothingly to your dog. Once he has calmed down, move on to the next nail. It is better to clip a little at a time, particularly with black-nailed dogs.

Hold your pup steady as you begin trimming his nails; you do not want him to make any sudden movements or run away. Talk to him soothingly and stroke him as you clip. Holding his foot in your hand, simply take off the end of each nail in one quick clip. You can purchase nail clippers that are specifically made for dogs; you can probably find them wherever you buy grooming supplies.

There are two predominant types of clippers. One is the guillotine clipper, which is a hole with a blade in the middle. Squeeze the handles, and the blade meets the nail and chops it off. It sounds gruesome, and for some dogs, it is intolerable. Scissor-type clippers are gentler on the nail. Just make sure the blades on either of these clippers are sharp. Once you are at the desired length, use a nail file to smooth the rough edges of the nails so they

don't catch on carpeting or debris outdoors.

If the procedure becomes more than you can deal with, just remember: Groomers and veterinarians charge a nominal fee to clip nails. By using their services you won't have to see your dog glower at you for the rest of the night.

When inspecting feet, you must check not only the nails but also the pads of the feet. Take care that the pads aren't cracked and always check between the pads to be sure that nothing has become lodged there. Depending upon the season, there may be a danger of grass seeds or thorns becoming embedded, or even tar from the road getting stuck. Butter, by the way, is useful to help remove tar from your pit bull's feet.

Did You Know?

The crunchiness of dry dog food helps keep teeth healthy and shiny by reducing plaque accumulation.

FLASH THOSE PEARLY WHITES

Like people, American Pit Bull Terriers can suffer from dental disease, so experts recommend regular teeth cleaning. Daily brushing is best, but your dog will benefit from a thorough teeth cleaning a few times a week. His teeth should be white and free of yellow tartar, and the gums should appear healthy and pink. Gums that bleed easily when you perform dental duties may have gingivitis.

The first thing to know is that your dog probably isn't going to want your fingers in his mouth. Desensitizing your pit bull — getting him to accept that you'll be looking at and touching his teeth — is the first step to overcoming his reticence. You can begin this as soon as you get your dog, with the help of something that motivates him most: food.

For starters, let your APBT lick some chicken, vegetable or beef broth off your finger. Then, dip your finger in broth again, and gently insert your finger in the side of your dog's mouth. Touch his side teeth and gums. Several sessions will get your dog used to having his mouth touched.

Use a toothbrush specifically made for a dog or a finger-tip brush wrapped around your finger to brush your American Pit Bull Terrier's teeth. Hold the mouth with one hand, and brush with the other. Use toothpaste made specifically for canines with dog-slurping flavors like poultry and beef. The human kind froths too much and can give your dog an upset stomach. Brush in a circular motion with the brush held at a 45-degree angle to the gum line. Be sure to get the fronts, tops and sides of each tooth.

Good dental hygiene promotes fresh breath, as well as a healthy heart.

Pay special attention to your
APBT's ears as they are a
common site for infections.

Look for signs of plaque, tartar or gum disease, including redness, swelling, foul breath, discolored enamel near the gum line and receding gums. If you see these, take your dog to the veterinarian immediately. Also see your vet about once a year for a dental checkup.

SHOW GROOMING

If your American Pit Bull is destined for the show ring, you may opt for a few finishing touches. Every dog can benefit from a bit of detail work but minimal grooming is the rule to maintain the breed's natural look. Your dog should be spotlessly clean, but the coat should feel smooth and stiff. Avoid shampoos that may soften the coat's natural texture. Timing can also make a difference. Some coats look and feel their best two or three days after a bath.

Trimming should enhance your APBT's smooth outline. Stray hairs can be removed from the outline of body, tip of tail and along the edges of cropped ears with thinning shears. Work slowly and stop frequently to evaluate the results. Don't overdo it or leave tell-tale straight lines or scissor marks in the coat. Whisker trimming is optional.

REWARD A JOB WELL DONE

Rewarding your pet for behaving during grooming is the best way to ensure stress-free grooming. Bathing energizes your pet, so using the time immediately after grooming to play is the best way to reward your pit bull for a job well done. Watching your clean, healthy APBT race from room to room out of sheer joy is *your* reward for being a smart owner!

Six Tips for APBT Care

1. Grooming tools can be scary to some dogs, so let yours see and sniff everything at the onset. Keep your beauty sessions short, too. Most bully breeds don't enjoy standing still for too long.

2. Look at your dog's eyes for any discharge, and his ears for inflammation, debris or foul odor. If you notice anything that doesn't look right, contact your veterinarian ASAP.

3. Choose a time to groom your dog when you don't have to rush, and assemble all of the grooming tools before you begin. This way, you can focus on your dog's needs instead of having to stop in the middle of the session.

4. Start establishing a grooming routine the day after you bring him home. A regular grooming schedule will make it easier to remember what touch-up tasks your dog needs.

5. Proper nail care will help with your dog's gait and spinal alignment. Nails that are too long can force a dog to walk improperly. Also, extra-long nails can snag and tear, causing painful injury to your American Pit Bull Terrier.

6. Good dental health prevents gum disease and early tooth loss. Brush your APBT's teeth daily and see a veterinarian yearly.

Six Questions to Ask a Groomer

1. Do you cage dry? Are you willing to hand dry or air dry my pet?

2. What type of shampoo are you using? Is it tearless? If not, do you have a tearless variety available for use?

3. Will you restrain my dog if he acts up for nail clipping? What methods do you use for difficult dogs?

4. Are you familiar with the American Pit Bull Terrier breed? Do you have any references from other pit bull owners?

5. Is the shop air-conditioned during hot weather?

6. Will my dog be getting brushed or just bathed?

TRAIN

American Pit Bull Terriers are strong, intelligent and tenacious. Tenacity is the positive side of stubborn, and with that innate blend of strength and will power; these bully breeds can be difficult to manage unless properly guided and trained.

Sara Gregware, a professional dog handler and trainer in Goshen, Conn., says of the bully types, "Their stubborn streak is incredible and their ability to tune you out is amazing." The harder these game-spirited dogs must work to win, the more excited and tenacious they become. Some people get frustrated by these dogs' will power and resort to harsh training, but that's a mistake. An escalating battle of will and muscle can cause lasting damage to the dog-and-handler relationship. These dogs are simply not quitters, even when strong punishment is involved. However, reward-based training works better despite these APBTs' hard-headedness or perhaps because of it.

Reward-based training methods — clicker and luring — show dogs what to do and help them do it correctly, setting them up for success and rewards rather than mistakes and

> **Did You Know?**
>
> **The prime period for socialization is short.** Most behavior experts agree that positive experiences during the 10-week period between 4 and 14 weeks of age are vital to the development of a puppy who'll grow into an adult dog with a sound temperament.

punishment. Most dogs find food rewards meaningful; APBTs are no exception. They tend to be very food-motivated. This works well because positive training relies on using treats, at least initially, to encourage the dog to demonstrate a behavior. The treat is then given as a reward. When you reinforce desired behaviors with rewards that are valuable to the dog, you are met with happy cooperation rather than resistance.

Positive reinforcement does not mean permissive. While you are rewarding your APBT's desirable behaviors, you must manage him to be sure he doesn't get rewarded for his undesirable behaviors. Training tools, such as leashes, tethers, baby gates and crates, help keep your dog out of trouble. The use of force-free negative punishment (the dog's behavior makes a good thing go away) helps him realize there are negative consequences for inappropriate behaviors.

LEARNING SOCIAL GRACES

Now that you have done all of the preparatory work and have helped your American Pit Bull Terrier get accustomed to his new home and family, it is time for a smart owner to have some fun! Socializing your tiny pup will give you the opportunity to show off your new friend, and your pit bull gets to reap the benefits of being an adorable little creature whom people will want to pet and, in general, think is absolutely precious!

Besides getting to know his new family, your puppy should be exposed to other people, animals and situations, but of course, he must not come into close contact with dogs who you don't know well until he has had all his vaccinations. This will help him become well-adjusted as he grows up and less prone to being timid or fearful of the new things he will encounter.

Your pup's socialization began at the breeder's home, but now it is your responsibility to continue it. The socialization he receives up until the age of 12 weeks is the most critical, as this is the time when he forms his impressions of the outside world. Be especially careful during the 8- to 10-week period, also known as the fear period. The interaction he receives during this time should be gentle and reassuring. Lack of socialization can manifest itself in fear and aggression as the dog grows up. The pup needs lots of human contact, affection, handling and exposure to other animals.

Once your APBT has received his necessary vaccinations, take him out and about (on his leash, of course). Walk him around the neighborhood, take him on errands, let people pet him and let him meet other dogs and pets. Expose your pit bull to different

SMART TIP!

If your pit bull refuses to sit with both haunches squarely beneath him and instead sits on one side or the other, he may have a physical reason for doing so. Discuss the habit with your veterinarian to be certain that your dog isn't suffering from some structural problem.

people — men, women, kids, babies, men with beards, teenagers with cell phones or riding skateboards, joggers, shoppers, someone in a wheelchair, a pregnant woman, etc. Make sure your APBT explores different surfaces like sidewalks, gravel and a puddle. Positive experience is the key to building confidence. It's up to you to make sure your APBT safely discovers the world so he will be calm, confident and well-socialized.

Training works best when blended into daily life. When your pit bull asks for something — food, play or whatever else — cue him to do something for you first. Reward him by granting his request. Practice in different settings, so your APBT will learn to listen regardless of his surroundings.

It's important that you take the lead in all socialization experiences and never put your pup in a scary or potentially harmful situation. Be mindful of your APBT's limitations. Fifteen minutes at a public market is fine; two hours at a loud outdoor concert is too much. Meeting vaccinated, tolerant and gentle older dogs is great. Meeting dogs whom you don't know isn't a great idea, especially if they appear very energetic, dominant or fearful. Control the situations in which you place your pup.

The best way to socialize your puppy to a new experience is to make him think it's the best thing ever. You can do this with a lot of happy talk, enthusiasm and, yes, food. To convince your puppy that almost any experience is a blast, always carry treats. Consider carrying two types — a bag of his puppy chow, which you can give him when introducing him to nonthreatening experiences, and a bag of high-value, mouth-watering treats to give him when introducing him to scarier experiences.

BASIC CUES

All APBTs, regardless of your training and relationship goals, need to know at least five basic good-manner behaviors: sit, down, stay, come and heel. Here are tips for teaching your dog these important cues.

SIT: Every dog should learn how to sit.
* Hold a treat at the end of your pit bull's nose.

Consistent training will lead to consistent results and success.

- Move the treat over his head.
- When he sits, click a clicker or say "Yes!"
- Feed your dog the treat.
- If your dog jumps up, hold the treat lower. If he backs up, back him into a corner and wait until he sits. Be patient. Keep your clicker handy, and click (or say "Yes!") and treat anytime he offers a sit.
- When he easily offers sits, say "sit" just before he offers, so he can make the association between the word and the behavior. Add the sit cue when you know you can get the behavior. Your dog doesn't know what the word means until you repeatedly associate it with the appropriate behavior.
- When your APBT sits easily on cue, start using intermittent reinforcement by clicking some sits but not others. At first, click most sits and skip an occasional one (this is a high rate of reinforcement). Gradually make your clicks more and more random.

DOWN: If your APBT can sit, then he can learn to lie down.
- ◆ Have your APBT sit.
- ◆ Hold the treat in front of his nose. Move it down slowly, straight toward the floor (toward his toes). If he follows all the way down, click and treat.
- ◆ If he gets stuck, slowly move the treat down. Click and treat for small movements downward — moving his head a bit lower or inching one paw forward. Keep clicking and treating until your APBT is all the way down. This is called "shaping" — rewarding small pieces of a behavior until your dog succeeds.

- ◆ If your dog stands as you move the treat toward the floor, have him sit, and move the treat more slowly downward, shaping with clicks and treats for small movements down as long as he is sitting. If he stands, cheerfully say "Oops!" (which means "Sorry, no treat for that!"), have him sit and try again.
- ◆ If shaping isn't working, sit on the floor with your knee raised. Have your APBT sit next to you. Put your hand with the treat under your knee and lure him under your leg so that he lies down and crawls to follow the treat. Click and treat!
- ◆ When you can lure the down easily, add the verbal cue, wait a few seconds to let your dog think, then lure him down to show him the association. Repeat until he'll go

Using food-motivated training techniques works well for APBTs.

down on the verbal cue. Then begin using intermittent reinforcement.

STAY: What good are sit and down cues if your dog doesn't stay?

▲ Start with your APBT in a sit or down position.

▲ Put the treat in front of your dog's nose and keep it there.

▲ Click and reward several times while he is in position, then release him with a cue that you will always use to tell him the

stay is over. Common release cues are: "all done," "break," "free," "free dog," "at ease" and "OK."

▲ When your APBT will stay in a sit or down position while you click and treat, add your verbal stay cue. Say "stay," pause for a second or two, click and say "stay" again. Release.

▲ When he's getting the idea, say "stay," whisk the treat out of sight behind your back, click and whisk the treat back. Be sure to get it all the way to his nose, so he does not jump up. Gradually increase the duration of the stay.

▲ When your American Pit Bull Terrier will stay for 15 to 20 seconds, add small distractions: shuffling your feet, moving your arms, small hops. Increase distractions gradually. If he makes mistakes, you're adding too much, too fast.

▲ When he'll stay for 15 to 20 seconds with distractions, gradually add distance. Have your dog stay, take a half-step back, click, return and treat. When he'll stay with a half-step, tell him to stay, take a full step back, click and return. Always return to your dog to treat after you click, but before you release. If you always return, his stay becomes strong. If you call him to you, his stay gets weaker due to his eagerness to come to you.

COME: A reliable recall — coming when called — can be a challenging behavior to teach. It is possible, however. To succeed, you need to install an automatic response to your "come" cue — one so automatic that your APBT doesn't even stop to think when he hears it, but will spin on his heels and charge to you at full speed.

▪ Start by charging a come cue the same way you charged your clicker. If your APBT already ignores the word "come," pick a different cue, like "front" or "hugs." Say your cue and feed him a bit of scrumptious treat. Repeat this until your pit bull's eyes light up when he hears the cue. Now you're ready to start training.

▪ With your APBT on a leash, run away several steps and cheerfully call out your charged cue. When he follows, click the clicker. Feed him a treat when he reaches you. For a more enthusiastic come, run away at full speed as you call him. When he follows at a gallop, click, stop running and give him a treat. The better your APBT gets at coming, the farther away he can be when you call him.

▪ Once your APBT understands the come cue, play with more people, each with a clicker and treats. Stand a short distance apart and take turns calling and running away. Click and treat in turn as he comes to each of you. Gradually increase the distance until he comes flying to each person from greater distances.

▪ When you and your APBT are ready to practice in wide-open spaces, attach a long

SMART TIP!

If you begin teaching the heel cue by taking long walks and letting the dog pull you along, he may misinterpret this action as an acceptable form of taking a walk. When you pull back on the leash to counteract his pulling, he will read that tug as a signal to pull even harder!

line — a 20- to 50-foot leash — to your dog, so you can gather up your APBT if that taunting squirrel nearby is too much of a temptation. Then, head to a practice area where there are less tempting distractions.

HEEL: Heeling means that the dog walks beside his owner without pulling. It takes time and patience on your part to succeed at teaching the dog that you will not proceed unless he is walking calmly beside you. Pulling out ahead on the leash is definitely not acceptable.

The "heel" command will make walks a pleasant experience for you both.

● Begin by holding the leash in your left hand as your APBT sits beside your left leg. Move the loop end of the leash to your right hand, but keep your left hand short on the leash so that it keeps your dog close to you.

● Say "heel" and step forward on your left foot. Keep your APBT close to you and take three steps. Stop and have the dog sit next to you in what is called the heel position. Praise verbally, but do not touch your dog. Hesitate a moment and begin again with "heel," taking three steps and stopping, at which point the dog is told to sit again.

Your goal here is to have your American Pit Bull Terrier walk those three steps without pulling on the leash. Once he will walk calmly beside you for three steps without pulling, increase the number of steps you take to five. When he will walk politely beside you while you take five steps, you can increase the length of your walk to 10 steps. Keep increasing the length of your stroll until your pit bull will walk quietly beside you without pulling for as long as you want him to heel. When you stop heeling, indicate to the dog that the

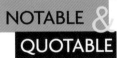

NOTABLE & QUOTABLE   *If you want to make your dog happy, create a digging spot where he's allowed to disrupt the earth. Encourage him to dig there by burying bones and toys, and helping him dig them up.* — Pat Miller, certified pet dog trainer and owner of Peaceable Paws dog-training facility in Hagerstown, Md.

Be sure to let your dog run and play after training sessions.

exercise is over by petting him and saying "OK, good dog." The "OK" is used as a release word, meaning that the exercise is finished, and he is free to relax.

● If you are dealing with an APBT who insists on pulling you around, simply put on your brakes and stand your ground until your APBT realizes that the two of you are not going anywhere until he is beside you and moving at your pace, not his. It may take some time just standing there to convince the dog that you are the leader, and you will be the one to decide on the direction and speed of your travel.

● Each time the dog looks up at you or slows down to give a slack leash between the two of you, quietly praise him and say, "Good heel. Good dog." Eventually, your APBT will begin to respond, and within a few days he will be walking politely beside you without pulling on the leash. At first, the training sessions should be kept short and very positive; soon the dog will be able to walk nicely with you for increasingly longer distances. Remember to give the dog free time and the opportunity to run and play when you have finished heel practice.

JOIN OUR ONLINE Club APBT®

The best way to get your pit bull well-socialized is to introduce him to different kinds of people and situations. Go online to download a socialization checklist at **DogChannel.com/Club-APBT**

TRAINING TIPS

If not properly socialized, managed and trained, even well-bred APBTs will exhibit undesirable behaviors such as jumping up, barking, chasing, chewing and other destructive behaviors. You can prevent these annoying habits and help your APBT become the perfect dog you're hoping for by following some basic training and behavior guidelines.

Be consistent. Consistency is important, not just in relation to what you allow your APBT to do (get on the sofa, perhaps) and not do (jump up on people), but also in the verbal and body language cues you use with your dog and in his daily routine.

Be gentle but firm. Positive training methods are very popular. Properly applied, dog-friendly methods are wonderfully effective, creating canine-human relationships based on respect and cooperation.

Manage behavior. All living things repeat rewarded behaviors. Behaviors that aren't reinforced will eventually go away.

Provide adequate exercise. A tired dog is a well-behaved dog. Many behavior problems can be avoided, others resolved, by providing your APBT with enough exercise.

THE THREE-STEP PROGRAM

Perhaps it's too late to give your dog consistency, training and management from the start. Maybe he came a pit bull rescue or a shelter, or you didn't realize the importance of these rules when he was a pup. He

SMART TIP!

It's a good idea to enroll in an obedience class if one is available in your area. Many areas have dog clubs that offer basic obedience training as well as preparatory classes for obedience competition. There are also local dog trainers who offer similar classes.

already may have learned some bad behaviors. Perhaps they're even part of his genetic package. Many problems can be modified with ease using the following three-step process for changing an unwanted behavior.

Step No. 1: Visualize the behavior you want from your dog. If you simply try to stop your APBT from doing something, you leave a behavior vacuum. You need to fill that vacuum with something, so your dog doesn't return to the same behavior or fill it with one that's even worse! If you're tired of your dog jumping up, decide what you'd prefer instead. A dog who greets people by sitting politely in front of them is a joy to own.

Step No. 2: Prevent your pit bull from being rewarded for the behavior you don't want. Management to the rescue! When your pit bull jumps up to greet you or get your attention, turn your back and step away to show him that jumping up no longer works to gain attention.

Step No. 3: Generously reinforce the desired behavior. Remember, dogs repeat behaviors that reward them. If your APBT no longer gets attention for jumping up and is

NOTABLE & QUOTABLE

I find that with the clicker, you are never dulling the drive of the dog; you just gently redirect the drive to your need. The dogs stay happy and learn fast — tails wagging, tongues lolling out of their silly expressions. — Robert MacBean, trainer and pit bull rescue volunteer in Burnaby, British Columbia

heavily reinforced with attention and treats for sitting, he will offer sits instead of jumping, because sits get him what he wants.

COUNTER CONDITIONING

Behaviors that respond well to the three-step process are those where the dog does something in order to get good stuff. He jumps up to get attention. He countersurfs because he finds good stuff on counters. He nips at your hands to get you to play with him.

The three steps don't work well when you're dealing with behaviors that are based in strong emotion, such as aggression and fear, or with hardwired behaviors such as chasing prey. With these, a smart owner can change the emotional or hardwired response through counter conditioning — programming a new emotional or automatic response to the stimulus by giving it a new association. Here's how you would counter condition an APBT who chases after skateboarders when you're walking him on a leash.

1. Have a large supply of very high-value treats, such as canned chicken.

2. Station yourself with your APBT on a leash at a location where skateboarders will pass by at a subthreshold distance "X" — that is, where your APBT alerts but doesn't lunge and bark.

3. Wait for a skateboarder. The instant your APBT notices the skateboarder, feed him bits of chicken, nonstop, until the skateboarder is gone.

4. Repeat many times until, when the skateboarder appears, your APBT looks at you with a big grin as if to say, "Yay! Where's my chicken?" This is a conditioned emotional response, or CER.

5. When you have a consistent CER at X, decrease the distance slightly, perhaps by 1 foot, and repeat until you consistently get the CER at this distance.

6. Continue decreasing the distance and obtaining a CER at each level, until a skateboarder zooming right past your American Pit Bull Terrier elicits the happy "Where's my chicken?" response. Now go back to distance X and add a second zooming skateboarder. Continue this process of gradual desensitization until your APBT doesn't turn a hair at a bevy of skateboarders.

LEAVE IT ALONE

Pit bulls enjoy eating, which makes it easy to train them using treats. But there's a downside to that gastronomic gusto — some APBTs gobble down anything even remotely edible. This could include fresh food, rotten food, things that once were food and any item that's ever been in contact with food. So, if you don't want your APBT gulping trash, teach him to leave things alone when told.

Many problem behaviors arise when puppies are taken away from the litter too early. Puppies learn a lot from their siblings.

Place a tempting tidbit on the floor and cover it with your hand (gloved against teeth, if necessary). Say your cue word ("Leave it" or "Nah"). Your dog might lick, nibble and paw your hand; don't give in or you'll be rewarding bad manners.

Wait until your dog moves away, then click or praise and give him a treat. Do not let your dog eat the temptation food that's on the floor, only the treats you give him. Repeat until your dog stops moving toward the food temptation.

Lift your hand momentarily, letting your dog see the temptation. Say the cue word.

Be ready to protect the treat but instantly reward your pit bull if he resists temptation. Repeat, moving your hand farther away and waiting longer before clicking and rewarding.

Increase the difficulty gradually — practice in different locations, add new temptations, drop treats from standing height, drop several at a time and step away.

Remember to use your cue word, so your dog will know what he's expected to do. Always reward good behavior! Rehearse this skill daily for a week. After that, you'll have enough real-life opportunities to practice.

BREAKING

BAD HABITS

Discipline — training one to act in accordance with rules — brings order to life. It is as simple as that. Without discipline, particularly in a group society, chaos reigns supreme and the group will eventually perish. Humans and canines are social animals and need some form of discipline in order to function effectively. Dogs need discipline in their lives in order to understand how their pack (you and other family members) functions and how they must act in order to survive.

Living with an untrained dog is a lot like owning a piano you don't know how to play; it's a nice object to look at but it doesn't do much else for you. Now begin taking piano lessons and suddenly the piano comes alive and brings forth magical sounds that set your heart singing and your body swaying.

The same is true with your American Pit Bull Terrier. Any dog is a big responsibility, and if not trained, may develop unacceptable behavior that annoys you or could even cause family friction.

Did You Know?

Anxiety can make a puppy miserable. Living in a world with scary monsters and suspected pit bull-eaters roaming the streets has to be pretty nerve-wracking. The good news is that timid dogs are not doomed to be forever ruled by fear. Owners who understand a timid American Pit Bull Terrier's needs can help him build self-confidence and a more optimistic view of life.

To train your APBT, you may enroll in an obedience class. There you can teach him good manners as you learn how and why he behaves the way he does. Find out how to communicate with your dog and how to recognize and understand how he communicates with you. Suddenly, your dog will take on a new role in your life; he is smart, interesting, well-behaved and fun to be with. He demonstrates his bond of devotion to you daily. In other words, your American Pit Bull Terrier does wonders for your ego because he constantly reminds you that you are not only his leader, you are his hero!

Those involved with teaching dog obedience and counseling owners about their dogs' behavior have discovered some interesting facts about dog ownership. For example, training dogs when they are puppies results in the highest success rate in developing well-mannered and well-adjusted adult dogs. Training an older dog, from 6 months to 6 years of age, can produce almost equal results providing that a smart owner accepts the dog's slower rate of learning capability and is willing to work patiently to help the dog succeed by developing to his fullest potential. Unfortunately, many owners of untrained adult dogs lack the patience, so they do not persist until their dogs are successful at learning particular behaviors.

Training a puppy aged 10 to 16 weeks (20 weeks at the most) is like working with a dry sponge in a pool of water. The pup soaks up whatever you show him and constantly looks for more things to do and learn. At this early age, his body is not yet producing hormones, therein lies the reason for such a high success rate. Without hormones, he is focused on his owners and not particularly interested in investigating other places, dogs, people, etc. You are his leader: his provider of food, water, shelter and security. He latches onto you and wants to stay close. He will usually follow you from room to room, will not let you out of his sight when you are outdoors with him and will respond in a similar manner to the people and animals you encounter. If you greet a friend warmly, he will be happy to greet the person as well. If, however, you are hesitant, even anxious, about the approach of a stranger, he will respond accordingly.

Once the puppy begins to produce hormones, his natural curiosity emerges and he begins to investigate the world around him. It is at this time when you may notice that the untrained dog begins to wander away from you and even ignore your commands to stay close.

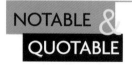

The best way to get through to dogs is through their stomach and mind — not the use of force. You have to play a mind game with them. — Sara Gregware, professional dog handler and trainer in Goshen, Conn.

There are usually classes within a reasonable distance of your home, but you also can do a lot to train your dog yourself. Whatever the circumstances, the key to successfully training your American Pit Bull Terrier without formal obedience classes lies within the pages of this book. This chapter is devoted to helping you train your APBT at home. If the recommended procedures are followed faithfully, you may expect positive results that will prove rewarding to you and your dog.

Whether your new charge is a puppy or a mature adult, the methods of teaching and the techniques used in training basic behaviors are the same. After all, no dog, whether puppy or adult, likes harsh or inhumane methods. All creatures, however, respond favorably to gentle motivational methods and sincere praise and encouragement.

The following behavioral problems are the ones that owners encounter the most. Every dog and situation is unique. Because behavioral abnormalities are the primary reason owners abandon their pets, we hope that you will make a valiant effort to train your American Pit Bull Terrier from the start.

NIP NIPPING

As puppies start to teethe, they feel the need to sink their teeth into everything; unfortunately, that includes your fingers, arms, hair, toes, whatever happens to be available. You may find this behavior cute for about the first five seconds — until you feel just how sharp those puppy teeth are.

Nipping is something you want to discourage immediately and consistently with a firm "No!" (or whatever number of firm "Nos" it takes for your dog to understand that you mean business) and replace your finger with an appropriate chew toy.

The golden rule of dog training is simple. For each "question" (cue), there is only one correct "answer" (reaction). One cue equals one reaction. Keep practicing the cue until your dog reacts correctly without hesitation. Be repetitive but not monotonous. Dogs get bored just as people do; a bored dog will not be focused on the lesson.

With proper training, a smart owner can teach their pit bull to stop jumping.

STOP THAT WHINING

A puppy will often cry, whine, whimper, howl or make some type of commotion when he is left alone. This is basically his way of calling out for attention, of calling out to make sure that you know he is there and that you have not forgotten about him. He feels insecure when he is left alone; for example, when you are out of the house and he is in his crate, or when you are in another part of the house and he cannot see you. The noise he is making is an expression of the anxiety he feels at being alone, so he needs to be taught that being alone is okay. You are not actually training the dog to stop making noise, you are training him to feel comfortable when he is alone and thus removing the need to make the noise.

This is where the crate with a cozy blanket and a toy comes in handy. You want to know that your pit bull pup is safe when you are not there to supervise, and you know that he will be safe in his crate rather than roaming freely about the house. In order for the pup to stay in his crate without making a fuss, he needs to be comfortable in his crate. On that note, it is extremely important that the crate is never used as a form of punishment, or your APBT will have a negative association with the crate.

Accustom the pup to the crate in short, gradually increasing intervals of time in

Keep training sessions short and sweet to keep your APBT enthusiastic about learning new things.

which you put him in the crate, maybe with a treat, and stay in the room with him. If he cries or makes a fuss, do not go to him, but stay in his sight. Gradually, he will realize that staying in his crate is all right without your help, and it will not be so traumatic for him when you are not around. You may want to leave the radio on softly when you leave the house; the sound of human voices can be comforting to him.

CHEW ON THIS

The national canine pastime is chewing! Every dog loves to sink his "canines" into a tasty bone, but most anything will do. Dogs need to chew to massage their gums, to make their new teeth feel better and to exercise their jaws. This is a natural behavior deeply imbedded in all things canine. Our role as owners is not to stop our dog from chewing, but to redirect it to positive, chew-

Did You Know?

Dogs do not understand our language. They can be trained, however, to react to a certain sound, at a certain volume. Never use your dog's name during a reprimand, as he might come to associate it with a bad thing!

Your pit bull may howl, whine or otherwise vocalize his displeasure at your leaving the house and his being left alone. This is a normal case of separation anxiety, but there are things that can be done to eliminate this problem. Your dog needs to learn that he will be fine on his own for a while and that he will not wither away if he isn't attended to every minute of the day.

In fact, constant attention can lead to separation anxiety in the first place. If you are endlessly coddling and cuddling your pit bull, he will come to expect this from you all of the time, and it will be more traumatic for him when you are not there.

To help minimize separation anxiety, make your entrances and exits as low-key as possible. Do not give your APBT a long, drawn-out good-bye, and do not lavish him with hugs and kisses when you return. This will only make him miss you more when you are away. Another thing you can try is to give your dog a treat when you leave; this will keep him occupied, it will keep his mind off the fact that you just left, and it will help him associate your leaving with a pleasant experience.

You may have to accustom your pit bull to being left alone in intervals, much like when you introduced him to his crate. Of course, when your dog starts whimpering as you approach the door, your first instinct will be to run to him and comfort him, but don't do it! Eventually, he will adjust and be just fine if you take it in small steps. His anxiety stems from being placed in an unfamiliar situation; by familiarizing him with being alone he will learn that he is OK. When your pit bull is alone in the house, confine him in his crate or a designated dog-proof area of the house. This should be the area in which he sleeps, so he will already feel comfortable there, and this should make him feel more at ease when he is alone. This is just one of the many examples in which a crate is an invaluable tool for you and your American Pit Bull Terrier, and another reinforcement of why your dog should view his crate as a happy place, a place of his own.

worthy objects. Be an informed owner and purchase proper chew toys for your pit bull, like strong nylon bones made for large dogs. Be sure that the devices are safe and durable, because your dog's safety is at risk.

The best answer is prevention: That is, put your shoes, handbags and other tasty objects in their proper places (out of the reach of the canine mouth). Direct puppies to their toys whenever you see them tasting the furniture legs or the leg of your pants. Make a noise to attract your American Pit Bull Terrier's attention and immediately escort him to his chew toy and engage him with the toy for at least four minutes, praising and encouraging him all the while.

NO MORE JUMPING

Jumping up is a dog's friendly way of saying hello! Some owners don't mind when their dog jumps up, which is fine for them. The problem arises when guests arrive and the dog greets them in the same manner — whether they like it or not! However friendly the greeting may be, the chances are that your visitors will not appreciate your dog's enthusiasm. The dog will not be able to distinguish between whom he can jump upon and whom he cannot. Therefore, it is probably best to discourage this behavior entirely.

Pick a command such as "Off" (avoid using "Down" because you will use that for the dog

to lie down) and tell him "Off" when he jumps up. Place him on the ground on all fours and have him sit, praising him the whole time. Always lavish him with praise and petting when he is in the sit position. That way you are still giving him a warm affectionate greeting, because you are as pleased to see him as he is to see you!

UNWANTED BARKING MUST GO

Barking is a dog's way of talking. It can be somewhat frustrating because it is not easy to tell what a dog means by his bark: is he excited, happy, frightened, angry? Whatever it is that the dog is trying to say, he should not be punished for barking. It is only when the barking becomes excessive, and when the excessive barking becomes a bad habit, that the behavior needs to be modified.

If an intruder came into your home in the middle of the night and your pit bull barked a warning, wouldn't you be pleased? You would probably deem your dog a hero, a wonderful guardian and protector of the home. On the other hand, if a friend drops by unexpectedly and rings the doorbell and is greeted with a sudden sharp bark, you would probably be annoyed at the dog. But isn't it just the same behavior? Your dog who doesn't know any better — unless he sees who is at the door and it is someone he is familiar with — will bark as a means of signaling to you that his (and your) territory is being threatened.

While your friend is not posing a threat, it's all the same to your American Pit Bull Terrier. Barking is his way of letting you know there is an intruder, whether friend or foe, on your property. This type of barking is instinctive and should not be discouraged.

Excessive habitual barking, however, is a problem that should be corrected early on. As your APBT grows up, you will be able to

SMART TIP!

Do not carry your puppy to his potty area. Lead him there on a leash, or better yet, encourage him to follow you to the spot. If you start carrying him, you might end up doing this routine for a long time and your dog will have the satisfaction of having trained you.

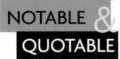

NOTABLE & QUOTABLE *Stage false departures. Pick up your car keys and put on your coat, then put them away and go about your routine. Do this several times a day, ignoring your dog while you do it. Soon his reaction to these triggers will decrease.*

— *September Morn, a dog trainer and behavior specialist in Bellingham, Wash.*

tell when his barking is purposeful and when it is for no reason. You will become able to distinguish his different barks and with what they are associated. For example, the bark when someone comes to the door will be different from the bark when he is excited to see you. It is similar to a person's tone of voice, except that the dog has to rely totally on tone of voice because he does not have the benefit of using words. An incessant barker will be evident at an early age.

There are some things that encourage a dog to bark. For example, if your dog barks nonstop for a few minutes and you give him a treat to quiet him, he believes that you are rewarding him for barking. He will associate barking with getting a treat and will keep doing it until he is rewarded.

FOOD STEALING AND BEGGING

Is your dog devising ways to steal food from your cupboards? If so, you must answer the following questions: Is your American Pit Bull Terrier really hungry? Why is there food on the coffee table? Face it, some dogs are more food-motivated than others; some dogs are totally obsessed by a slab of brisket and can only think of their next meal. Food stealing is terrific fun and always yields a great reward — food, glorious food!

The owner's goal, therefore, is to make the reward less rewarding, even startling! Plant a shaker can (an empty can with coins inside) on the table so that it catches your pooch off-guard. There are other devices available that will surprise the dog when he is looking for a mid-afternoon snack. Such remote-control devices, though not the first choice of some trainers, allow the correction to come from the object instead of the owner. These devices are also useful to keep the snacking hound from napping on furniture.

Just like food stealing, begging is a favorite pastime of hungry puppies with that same reward — food! Dogs quickly learn that humans love that feed-me pose and that their selfish owners keep the "good food" for themselves. Why would humans dine on kibble when they can cook up sausages and kielbasa? Begging is a conditioned response related to a specific stimulus, time and place. The sounds of the kitchen, cans and bottles opening, crinkling bags and the smell of food being prepared will excite the chowhound and soon the paws are in the air!

Here is the solution to stop this behavior: Never give in to a beggar, no matter how cute or desperate! You are rewarding the dog for sitting pretty, jumping up, whining and rubbing his nose into you by giving him that glorious reward — food. By ignoring the dog, you will (eventually) force the behavior into extinction. Note that the behavior likely will get worse before it disappears, so be sure there aren't any softies in the family who will give in to your dog when he whimpers, "More, please."

DIG THIS

Digging, which is seen as a destructive behavior to humans, is actually quite a natural behavior in dogs and their desire to dig can be irrepressible and most frustrating to owners. When digging occurs in your yard, it is actually a normal behavior redirected into something the dog can do in his everyday life. In the wild, a dog would be actively seeking food, making his own shelter, etc. He would be using his paws in a purposeful manner for his survival. Because you provide him with food and shelter, he has no need to use his paws for these purposes, and so the energy that he would be using may manifest itself in the form of little holes all over your yard and flower beds.

Perhaps your dog is digging as a reaction to boredom — it is somewhat similar to someone eating a whole bag of chips in front of the TV — because they are there and there is nothing better to do! Basically, the answer is to provide the dog with adequate play and exercise so that his mind and paws are occupied, and so that he feels as if he is doing something useful.

Of course, digging is easiest to control if it is stopped as soon as possible, but it is often hard to catch a dog in the act. If your dog is a compulsive digger and is not easily distracted by other activities, you can designate an area on your property where it is OK for him to dig. If you catch him digging in an off-limits area of the yard, immediately bring him to the approved area and praise him for digging there. Keep a close eye on him so that you can catch him in the act; that is the

Did You Know?

Some natural remedies for separation anxiety are reputed to have calming effects, but check with your vet before use. Flower essence remedies are water-based extracts of different plants, which are stabilized and preserved with brandy. A human dose is only a few drops, so seek advice from a natural healing practitioner on proper dosage for your pit bull.

only way to make him understand what is permitted and what is not. If you take him to a hole he dug an hour ago and tell him "No," he will understand that you are not fond of holes, or dirt, or flowers. If you catch him while he is stifle-deep in your tulips, that is when he will get your message.

POOP ALERT!

Humans find feces eating, aka *coprophagia*, one of the most disgusting behaviors that their dog could engage in; yet to the dog, it is perfectly normal. Vets have found that diets with a low digestibility, containing relatively low levels of fiber and high levels of starch, increase *coprophagia*. Therefore, high-fiber diets may decrease the likelihood of dogs eating feces. To discourage this behavior in your American Pit Bull Terrier, feed food that is nutritionally complete and in the proper amount. If changes in his diet do not seem to work, and no medical cause can be found, you will have to modify the behavior through environmental control before it becomes a habit.

There are some tricks you can try, such as adding an unpleasant-tasting substance to the feces to make them unpalatable or

Contrary to media portrayals, American Pit Bull Terriers are fun-loving, loyal and great companions.

adding something to the dog's food which will make it unpleasant tasting after it passes through the dog. The best way to prevent your dog from eating his stool is to make it unavailable — clean up after he eliminates and remove any stool from the yard. If it is not there, he cannot eat it.

Never reprimand your dog for stool eating, as this rarely impresses him. Vets recommend distracting a dog while he is in the act of stool eating. Another option is to muzzle him when he is in the yard to relieve himself; this usually is effective within 30 to 60 days. *Coprophagia* most frequently is seen in pups 6 to 12 months of age, and usually disappears around the dog's first birthday.

AGGRESSION

Aggression can be a very big problem in dogs. Aggression, when not controlled, becomes dangerous. An aggressive dog, no matter the size, may lunge at, bite or even attack a person or another dog. This type of behavior is not to be tolerated. It is more than just inappropriate behavior; it is not safe, especially with a powerful breed such as the pit bull. It is painful for a family to watch their dog become unpredictable in his behavior to the point where they are afraid of the dog. And while not all aggressive behavior is dangerous, it can be frightening: growling, baring teeth, etc. It is important to get to the root of the problem to ascertain why the dog is acting in this manner. Aggression is a display of dominance, and the dog should not have the dominant role in his pack, which, in this case, is your family.

It is important not to challenge an aggressive dog as this could provoke an attack. Observe your pit bull's body language. Does he make direct eye contact and stare? Does he try to make himself as large as possible: ears pricked, chest out, tail erect? Height and size signify authority in a dog pack; being taller or above another dog literally means that he is above in the social status. These body signals tell you that your pit bull thinks he is in charge, a problem that needs to be dealt with. An aggressive dog is unpredictable in that you never know when he is going to strike and what he is going to do. You cannot understand why a dog that is playful and loving one minute is growling and snapping the next.

Fear is a common cause of aggression in dogs. If you can isolate what brings out the fear reaction, you can help the dog get over it. Supervise your pit bull's interactions with people and other dogs, and praise the dog when it goes well. If he starts to act aggressively in a situation, correct him and remove him from the situation. Do not let people approach the dog and start petting him without your express permission. That way, you can have the dog sit to accept petting, and praise him when he behaves properly. You are focusing on praise and on modifying his behavior by rewarding him when he acts appropriately. By being gentle and by supervising his interactions, you are showing him that there is no need to be afraid or defensive.

The best solution is to consult a behavioral specialist, one who has experience with the pit bull if possible. Together, perhaps you can pinpoint the cause of your dog's aggression and do something about it. An aggressive dog cannot be trusted, and a dog who cannot be trusted is not safe to have as a family pet. If the pet pit bull becomes untrustworthy, he cannot be kept in the home with the family. The family must get rid of the dog. In the very worst case, the dog must be euthanized.

AGGRESSION TOWARD OTHER DOGS

A pit bull's aggressive behavior toward another dog stems from the breed's fighting-dog ancestry as well as from not enough exposure to other dogs at an early age. If other dogs make your pit bull nervous and agitated, he will lash out as a protective mechanism. A dog who has not received sufficient exposure to other canines tends to believe that he is the only dog on the planet. The animal becomes so dominant that he does not even show signs that he is fearful or threatened. Without growling or any other physical signal as a warning, he will lunge at and bite the other dog.

A way to correct this is to let your pit bull approach another dog when walking on leash. Watch very closely and at the very first sign of aggression, correct your pit bull and pull him away. Scold him for any sign of discomfort, and then praise him when he ignores or tolerates the other dog. Keep this up until either he stops the aggressive behavior, learns to ignore the other dog or even accepts other dogs. Praise him lavishly for his correct behavior.

DOMINANT AGGRESSION

A social hierarchy is firmly established in a wild dog pack. The dog wants to dom-

inate those under him and please those above him. Dogs know that there must be a leader. If you are not the obvious choice for emperor, the dog will assume the throne! These conflicting innate desires are what a dog owner is up against when he sets about training a dog. In training a dog to obey commands, the owner is reinforcing that he is the top dog in the "pack" and that the dog should, and should want to, serve his superior. Thus, the owner is suppressing the dog's urge to dominate by modifying his behavior and making him obedient.

An important part of training is taking every opportunity to reinforce that you are the leader. The simple action of making your pit bull sit to wait for his food instead of allowing him to run up to get it when he wants it says that you control when he eats; he is dependent on you for food. Although it may be difficult, do not give in to your dog's wishes every time he whines at you or looks at you with pleading eyes. It is a constant effort to show the dog that his place in the pack is at the bottom.

This is not meant to sound cruel or inhumane. You love your pit bull and you should treat him with care and affection. You (hopefully) did not get a dog just so you could control another creature. Dog training is not about being cruel or feeling important, it is about molding the dog's behavior into what is acceptable and teaching him to live by your rules. In theory, it is quite simple: catch him in appropriate behavior and reward him for it.

With a dominant dog, punishment and negative reinforcement can have the opposite effect of what you are after. It can make a dog fearful and/or act out aggressively if he feels he is being challenged. Remember, a dominant dog perceives him-

self at the top of the social heap and will fight to defend his perceived status. The best way to prevent that is to never give him reason to think that he is in control in the first place.

If you are having trouble training your pit bull and it seems as if he is constantly challenging your authority, enlist an obedience trainer or behavioral specialist. A professional will work with you and your dog to teach you effective training techniques to use at home. Beware of trainers who rely on excessively harsh methods; scolding is necessary now and then, but

the focus of your training should always be on positive reinforcement.

SEXUAL BEHAVIOR

Dogs exhibit certain sexual behaviors that may have influenced your choosing a male or female when you first purchased your pit bull. Spaying/neutering will eliminate most of these behaviors, but if you are purchasing a dog who you wish to show or breed, you should be aware of what you will have to deal with during the dog's life.

Females usually have two estruses per year, each season lasting about three weeks. These are the only times in which she will mate, and she usually will not allow this until the second week of the cycle. If she is not bred during the heat cycle, it is not uncommon for her to experience a false pregnancy, in which her mammary glands swell and she exhibits maternal tendencies toward her toys.

Owners must also recognize that mounting, a common behavior, is not merely a sexual expression but also a way of displaying dominance. Be consistent as well as persistent, and you will find that you can "move mounters."

CHAPTER 12

THE PLAYFUL

PIT BULL

hether a pit bull is trained in the structured environment of a class or alone with his owner at home, there are many activities that can bring fun and rewards to smart owners and their dogs once they have mastered basic obedience commands.

Teaching your dog to help out around the home, in the garden or on the farm provides great satisfaction for both of you. In addition, your APBT's help will make life a little easier, raise his stature as a valued companion to his family, gives him a purpose, helps to keep his mind occupied and provides an outlet for his energy.

If you are interested in participating in organized competition with your pit bull, try one of the following activities.

EXERCISE OPTIONS

All dogs need exercise to keep them physically and mentally healthy. An inactive dog is a fat dog, with the accompanying likelihood of joint strain or torn ligaments. Inactive dogs also are prone to mischief — and may do anything to relieve their boredom. This often leads to behavior problems such as chewing or barking. Regular daily exercise like daily walks and short play sessions will help keep your American Pit Bull Terrier slim, trim and happy.

Did You Know?

The Fédération Internationale Cynologique is the world kennel club that governs dog shows around the world.

Before You Begin

Because of the physical demands of sporting activities, an APBT puppy should not begin officially training until she is done growing. That doesn't mean that you can't begin socializing her to sports, though. Talk to your vet about what age is appropriate to begin training.

Provide your American Pit Bull Terrier with interactive play that stimulates his mind as well as his body. It's a good idea to have a daily period of one-on-one play, especially with a puppy or young dog. Continue this type of interaction throughout your dog's life, and you will build a lasting bond. Even seniors who are slowing down a bit need the stimulation activity provides.

If your APBT is older or overweight, consult your veterinarian about how much and what type of exercise he needs. Usually, a 10- to 15-minute walk once a day is a good start. As the pounds start to drop off, your dog's energy level will rise, and you can increase the amount of daily exercise.

Lots of activities are out there — competitive or otherwise. Overall, though, they want to do things with you. As long as you're aware of your environment and your pit bull's social behavior, you can provide him with the active lifestyle he deserves.

OBEDIENCE TRIALS

Obedience trials in the United States trace back to the early 1930s, when organized obedience was developed to demonstrate how well dogs and owners could work together. The pioneer of obedience was Helen Whitehouse Walker, a Standard Poodle fancier, who designed a series of exercises after the Associated Sheep, Police and Army Dog Society of Great Britain. Since the days of Walker, obedience trials have grown by leaps and bounds, and today more than 2,000 trials are held in the United States every year, with more than 100,000 dogs competing.

Competitive obedience takes the basics and expands them into specific exercises you and your pit bull must perform correctly in order to "qualify." In each of the three classes — novice, open and utility — your team starts with a perfect 200 score and loses points for various imperfections. Qualifying requires a minimum score of 170, with three passing scores under two different judges necessary for a title.

Exercises include heeling, jumping, coming on cue stay, scent work and more. Judges look for exactness in execution, a happy, willing worker and an "in sync" relationship between owner and dog. Though this joyful attitude proved difficult to achieve with punishment based training, modern motivational techniques place it within easy reach.

However, not every obedience facility welcomes APBTs with open arms, often due to local legislations. It may take some effort to find one that accepts the breed. Ask your veterinarian, check local phone listings under "pets" or "dog training," and do an Internet search for possible trainers. Private lessons might end up your sole option, well worth the expense unless you possess considerable training experience.

Training methods vary widely, but most contemporary instructors employ motivational, positive techniques that encourage rather than force cooperation. Treats, toys, play and praise help the dog learn without intimidation. However, this should be coupled with consistency and definite rules, like expecting compliance on a learned command first time, every time.

NOTABLE & QUOTABLE *Pit bulls excel at meeting strangers. They haven't met anyone they haven't known before. One of my dogs, Alex, was rescued from a drug raid and had a really bad start in life, but she's always been able to zero in on the people who needed her affection most.* — Cydney Cross, president of Out of the Pits, an animal rescue and education organization supporting pit bulls based in Old Chadham, N.Y.

AGILITY TRIALS

Agility is one of the most popular dog sports out there. Training your American Pit Bull Terrier in agility will boost his confidence, teach him to focus on you and keep him active.

In agility competition, the dog and the handler move through a prescribed course, negotiating a series of obstacles that may include jumps, tunnels, a dog walk, an A-frame, a seesaw, a pause table and weave poles. Dogs who run through a course without refusing any obstacles, going off course or knocking down any bars, all within a set time, receive a qualifying score. Dogs with a certain number of qualifying scores in their given division — which depend on experience and physical size — earn an agility title.

Several different organizations recognize agility events. AKC-sanctioned agility events are the most common. The United States Dog Agility Association, based in Dallas, Texas, also sanctions agility trials, as does the United Kennel Club. The rules are different for each of these organizations, but the principles are the same.

When your American Pit Bull Terrier starts his agility training, he will begin by learning to negotiate each individual obstacle while on the leash, as you guide him. Eventually, you will steer him through multiple obstacles in a row, one after another. Once he catches on that this is how agility works, he can run a short course off the leash. One day, you will see the light go on in your American Pit Bull Terrier's eyes as he figures out that he should look to you for guidance as he runs through the agility course. Your job will be to tell him which obstacles to take next, by using your voice and your body as signals.

RALLY BEHIND RALLY

Rally is a sport that combines competition obedience with elements of agility, but is less demanding than either one of these activities. Rally was designed with the average dog owner in mind, and is easier than many other sporting activities.

Agility offers jumps, tunnels, chutes, platforms and more fun stuff than you can imagine.

At a rally event, dogs and handlers are asked to move through 10 to 20 different stations, depending on the level of competition. They are marked by signs, which tell the handler the exercise to be performed at each station. The exercises vary from making different types of turns to changing pace.

Dogs can earn rally titles as they get better at the sport and move through the different levels. The titles to strive for are Rally Novice, Rally Advanced, Rally Excellent and Rally Advanced Excellent.

To get your American Pit Bull Terrier puppy prepared to do rally competition, focus

on teaching him basic obedience, for starters. Your dog must know the five basic obedience cues — sit, down, stay, come and heel — and perform them well before he's ready for rally. Next, you can enroll your dog in a rally class. Although he must be at least 6 months of age to compete in rally, you can start training long before his 6-month birthday.

SHOW DOGS

When you purchase your American Pit Bull Terrier puppy, you must make it clear to the breeder whether you want one just as a lovable companion and pet, or if you hope to be buying an American Pit Bull Terrier with show prospects. No reputable breeder will sell you a puppy and tell you that the dog will definitely be show quality because so much can go wrong during the early months of a puppy's development. If you do plan to show, what you hopefully will have acquired is a puppy with show potential.

To the novice, exhibiting an American Pit Bull Terrier in the ring may look easy, but it takes a lot of hard work and devotion to win at a major day show, not to mention a little luck, too!

The first concept that the canine novice learns when watching a dog show is that each dog first competes against members of his own breed. Once the judge has selected the best member of each breed (Best of Breed) the chosen dog will compete with other dogs in his group. Finally, the dogs chosen first in each UKC group will compete for Best In Show.

The second concept a beginner must understand is that the dogs are not actually compared against one another. The judge compares each dog against the breed standard, the written description of the ideal specimen that is approved by the kennel club. While some early breed standards were indeed based on specific dogs who were famous or popular, many dedicated enthusiasts say that a perfect specimen as described in the standard has never walked into a show ring, has never been bred and, to the woe of dog breeders around the globe, does not exist. Breeders attempt to get as close to this ideal as possible with every litter, but theoretically the "perfect" dog is so elusive it is impossible to find. (And if the perfect dog were born, breeders and judges probably would never agree that he was indeed perfect.)

If you are interested in exploring the world of conformation, your best bet is to join your local breed club or the national (or parent) club, the National American Pit Bull Terrier Association. These clubs often host regional and national specialties, shows open only to American Pit Bull Terriers, which can include conformation as well as obedience and field trials. Even if you have no intention of competing with your American Pit Bull Terrier, a specialty is a like a festival for lovers of the breed who congregate to share their favorite topic: American Pit Bull Terriers! Clubs also send out newsletters, and some organize training days and seminars in order that people may learn more about their chosen breed. To locate the breed club closest to you, contact

SMART TIP!

If you find your pit bull isn't suited for group activities, once you get your veterinarian's OK and basic obedience training behind you, you and your bully breed can also find plenty of opportunities in your own backyard for exercise and training to strengthening the bond between you and your APBT.

High-energy APBTs are often good candidates for specialized training.

the UKC, which creates the rules and regulations for these events, plus dog registration and other basic dog-ownership requirements.

THERAPY TERRIERS

Therapy work offers a special kind of satisfaction, the gratification of bringing pleasure simply through your dog's presence. If you like helping people, you and your American Pit Bull Terrier can bring happiness and laughter to people who are confined to hospitals and nursing homes. Therapy-dog visits are a wonderful way for you to share the enjoyment of American Pit Bull Terrier ownership with others. Petting your dog can ease the loneliness of a widower in a nursing home, lower the blood pressure of a hospital patient and win big grins and laughs from children in a cancer ward.

Your therapy American Pit Bull Terrier must be clean, flea-free and exhibit good manners. No food stealing or potty accidents! He must pass a temperament test to ensure that he's suited to this type of work.

A sweet, tolerant, fearless disposition is ideal because therapy work involves encounters with new or unusual places, people and equipment. Both you and your American Pit Bull Terrier will attend training classes before visits begin. Be sure to take normal precautions against falls from aged, shaky hands or run-ins with wheelchairs or walkers. A short leash attached to a harness will help you keep control.

CANINE GOOD CITIZEN

If obedience work sounds too regimented but you'd still like your American Pit Bull

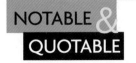
NOTABLE & QUOTABLE

This breed is the ultimate athlete, able to perform a variety of tasks well. They are the stand-out breed in weight pulling, easily handling the jumping and maneuvering of agility, and work capably at obedience. — National American Pit Bull Terrier Association president Michael Snyder of Seattle, Wash.

it's a Fact American Pit Bull Terriers account for nearly half of the more than 30 dogs currently holding United Kennel Club Superdog status.

Terrier to have a title, prepare him for the Canine Good Citizen test. This program is sponsored by the AKC, with tests administered by local dog clubs, private trainers and 4-H clubs.

To earn a CGC title, your American Pit Bull Terrier must be well-groomed and demonstrate the manners that all good dogs should exhibit. The CGC test requires a dog to perform the sit, down, stay and come commands; react appropriately to other dogs and distractions; allow a stranger to approach him; sit politely for petting; walk nicely on a loose leash; move through a crowd without going wild; calm down after play or praise; and sit still for examination by the judge. Rules are posted on www.akc.org or go to DogChannel.com/Club-APBT and click on "Downloads" for more information.

WEIGHT PULLING

Just as many people lift weights to keep themselves in peak condition, many pit bull owners like to keep their dogs in peak condition as well. These smart owners may be interested in involving their dogs in regular weight-pulling exercises.

Before discussing weight-pulling exercises for your dog, you should understand a few things. The first is that the pit bull breed is not and has never been a weight-pulling dog. This is to say that weight pulling was never an activity for which this breed was selectively bred. Other breeds were, and continue to be, selectively bred for their ability to pull weights; sled dogs being the best example of such breeds.

United Kennel Club super dogs to the rescue!

With poor breeding practices and irresponsible ownership spurring negative press and breed-specific legislations, saving the American Pit Bull Terrier may require nothing short of heroic efforts. Fortunately, United Kennel Club "super-dogs," like Valerie Piltz's multi-titled pit bull Klicker, valiantly work to show the world what this breed can do in the right hands.

Though she says the title hasn't yet gained official status, Piltz, a conformation and weight pull judge from Bellevue, Wash., defines a superdog as a UKC registered conformation champion from any breed that earns a title in obedience, agility and weight pulling. Every title necessitates three qualifying scores per each competitive level, with each level demanding progressively more complex skills.

According to Piltz, another trait that contributes strongly to super-dog success comes from the breed's absolute willingness to please his owner. This attribute explains the APBT's consistent wins in weight-pull events, where the owner's verbal encouragement — never force — brings the dog to the finish line.

Andrew Yori of Rochester, Minn., says that drive proves an important characteristic in turning a high-energy dog into an athletic superstar. In training, this relates to the dog's intensity, keenness and determination toward earning a reward. Yori successfully channeled his rescued pit bull Wallace's drive into disc dog events, winning the Purina Incredible Dog Challenge Freestyle Flying Disc competition in 2007.

Nonetheless, there is nothing fundamentally wrong with involving your pit bull in weight pulls for fun, sport and exercise. Due to the association of the pit bull breed with the activity of dog fighting, other dog fanciers may misinterpret or resent your interest in this activity.

Should you decide to begin training your pit bull for weight pulling, you will need a few things. First, you probably will want an indoor location. Second, you will need some carpeting so your dog won't hurt his paws while pulling. A carpet that is not very plush is best for this; indoor/outdoor carpeting is ideal. Third, you will need a cart with wheels and a low flat top. Such a cart can be easily built. It should not be very wide and the wheels should be 6 or so inches in diameter. Larger wheels will make for an easier pull. If you want to get serious about weight-pulling competitions, find a local club that sponsors weight-pulling events for dogs and be sure to construct a cart that meets the club's competition standards.

Fourth, you will need weights. Bricks or cinder blocks are fine, but the kind of weightlifting plates people use are best. If you are a weightlifter, you will not need to purchase additional weights; if not, the weights can be purchased from a sporting-goods store.

Finally, you will need a harness to attach the cart to the dog. Such harnesses are often available through magazines that cater to pit bull owners, but a comfortable leather harness can also be made by a leather worker who deals with horses. If you intend to have a harness made just for weight pulling, start the dog off wearing the harness before you introduce the animal to pulling weights. Allow the dog time to associate the harness with positive events like a short walk. Once the dog is comfortable with the harness, or with one like it, you can begin to use the harness for cart pulling.

It's best to have two people present during weight-pulling exercises. Begin by harnessing your dog to the cart with no weights on the cart. Have a friend (one who knows your dog and with whom your dog is familiar) hold the harnessed dog on the carpet while you take a position a few yards in front. Simultaneously release your dog and begin to encourage him to come to you. If your dog looks confused and does not move, encourage him more. If he refuses to come, end the session and try again another day. You might also try sitting in your position, acting casual and waiting for him to come to you. Often a little gentle encouragement is easier to comprehend than an overwhelming onslaught of encouragement.

When your American Pit Bull Terrier finally pulls the empty cart in order to come to you, act excited and praise him profusely. Try the pull again and again. Use no weights on the first day of pulling unless your dog is obviously enjoying himself, which some dogs do. As your dog becomes familiar with the routine, begin to add weight to the cart. Start off with light weights and, when your dog has learned to pull these with enthusiasm, begin an actual training routine.

OTHER SPORTS

Thanks to the American Pit Bull Terrier's multi-tasking skills, there are plenty of other sports in which he can excel.

Backpacking: Backpacking provides an excellent conditioning activity that burns canine energy while you enjoy a healthy hike. Dogs need properly fitted equipment to prevent discomfort and chafing as they carry water, snacks or their own food for overnight trips. Several organizations offer backpacking titles, including the Dog Scouts of America.

Dockdogs: A thrilling sport for a pit bull that like water, a dockdog leaps off a dock of specified proportions to retrieve a toy thrown by his handler. The length of the jump is measured from the edge of the dock to where the dog's rump hits the water, not including the tail. The Dockdog organization offers titling.

Tracking: This fascinating outdoor activity entails training your APBT to follow a specific human scent for various distances. Tracks are usually aged anywhere from 20 minutes to several hours, with "lost" articles dropped along the trail for your dog to locate. Titles can be earned through various organizations, such as Schutzhund USA.

Carting, Sledding, Skijoring, Scootering: Different approaches to pulling sports, each of these activities utilize your APBT's strength and desire to pull coupled with firm obedience. The latter seems logical since the dog generally pulls along a human. Carting offers the most likelihood for titling, the rest provide great exercise and fun.

A smart APBT owner will find a sport both he and his pit bull can enjoy.

CHAPTER 13

RESOURCES

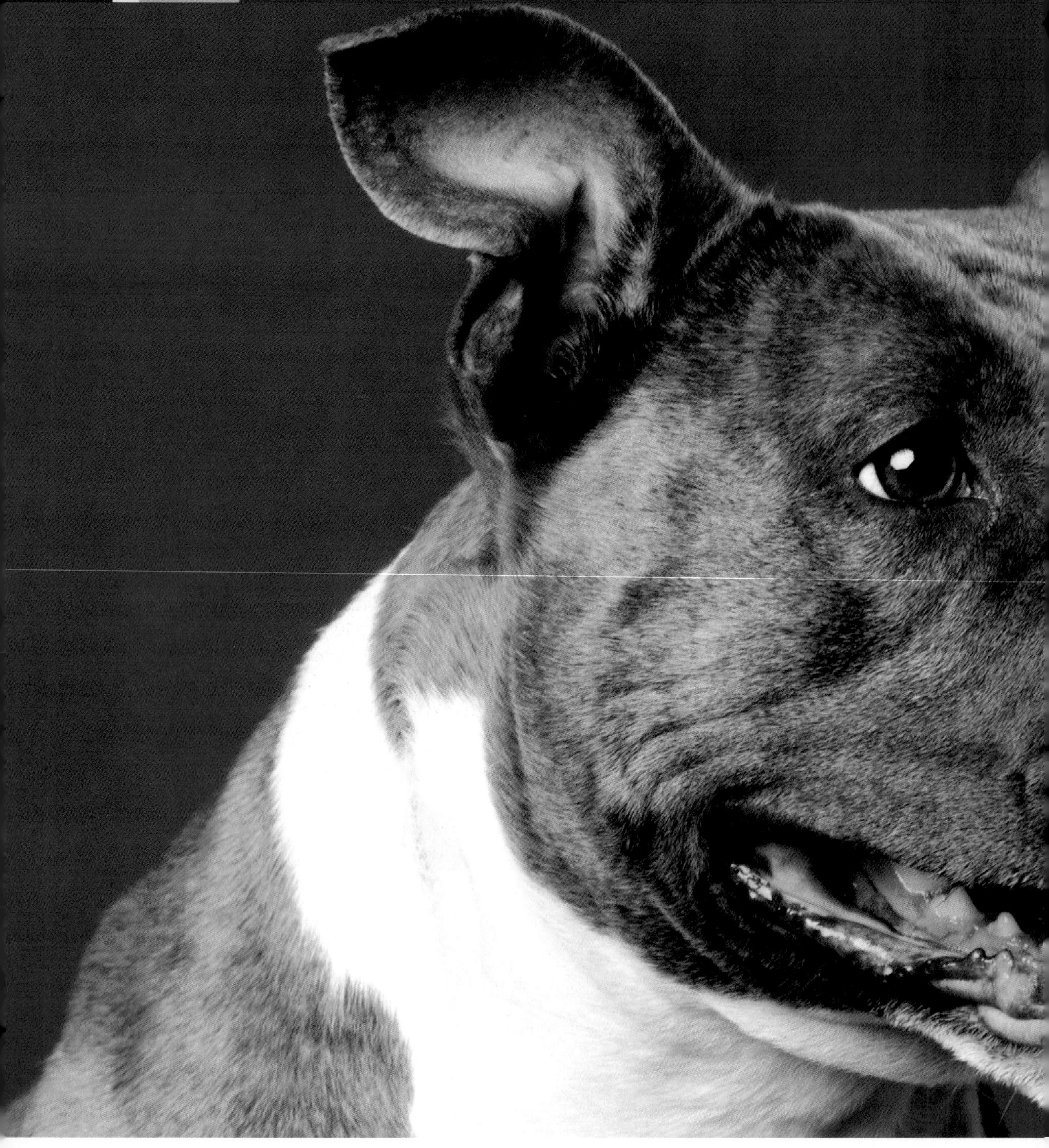

To find more information about pit bulls, contact the following organizations. They will be glad to help you dig deeper into the world of APBTs.

American Kennel Club: The AKC website offers information and links to conformation, tracking, rally, obedience and agility programs, and member clubs. The AKC registers American Staffordshire Terriers instead of APBTs. www.akc.org

BAD RAP (Bay Area Dog lovers Responsible About Pit Bulls): This organization finds homes for rescued pit bulls. www.badrap.org

Canadian Kennel Club: The CKC follows the AKC and registers American Staffordshire Terriers instead of APBTs. www.ckc.ca

International Weight Pulling Association: This great dog sport gives dogs a job to do. www.iwpa.net

Love on a Leash: More than 900 members are involved in this pet therapy organization. www.loveonaleash.org

Misunderstood Pit Bull Rescue: This organization finds homes for rescued pit bulls. www.misunderstood.rescuegroups.org

it's a
Fact

The **American Kennel Club** was started in 1884. It is America's oldest kennel club. The **United Kennel Club** is the second oldest in the United States. It began registering dogs in 1898. The first UKC breed registered was the American Pit Bull Terrier.

National American Pit Bull Terrier Association: The national APBT club. www.napbta.com

North American Dog Agility Council: This site provides links to clubs, trainers, and agility trainers in the United States and Canada. www.nadac.com

Pit Bull Rescue Central: This organization helps find homes for rescued pit bulls. www.pbrc.net

Spindletop Pit Bull Refuge: This organization also pairs rescued pit bulls with loving owners. www.spindletoppitbullrefuge.org

Staffordshire Terrier Club of America: He's a cousin of the APBT. www.amstaff.org

Therapy Dogs Inc.: Get your APBT involved in therapy. www.therapydogs.com

Therapy Dogs International: Find more therapy dog info here: www.tdi-dog.org

United Kennel Club: The UKC offers several of the events also offered by the AKC, including agility, conformation and obedience. In addition, the UKC organizes competitions in hunting and dog sport (companion and protective events). The UKC and the AKC offer programs for junior handlers, ages 2 to 18. www.ukcdogs.com

United States Dog Agility Association: The USDAA has information on training, clubs and events in the United States, Canada, Mexico and overseas. www.usdaa.com

Villalobos Rescue Center: This Canyon Country, Calif., organization helps find homes for rescued American Pit Bull Terriers and pit bull mixes. www.vrcpitbull.com

World Canine Freestyle Organization: Dancing with your dog is fun! www.worldcaninefreestyle.org

BOARDING

So you want to take a family vacation, and you want to include all members of the family. You usually make arrangements for accommodations ahead of time anyway, but this is imperative when traveling with a pit bull. You do not want to make an overnight stop at the only place around for miles and find out that the hotel doesn't allow dogs. Also, you do not want to reserve a room for your family without confirming that you are traveling with a pit bull because, if it is against the hotel's policy, you may not have a place to stay.

Alternatively, if you are traveling and choose not to bring your APBT, you will have to make arrangements for him. Some options are to bring him to a family member or a neighbor, have a trusted friend stop by often, stay at your house or bring your dog to a reputable boarding kennel.

If you choose to board him at a kennel, visit in advance to see the facilities and check how clean they are and where the dogs are kept. Talk to some of the employees and see how they treat the dogs; do they spend time with the dogs, play with them, exercise them, etc.? Also, find out the kennel's policy on vaccinations and what they require. This is for all of the dogs' safety because when dogs are kept together, there is a greater risk of diseases being passed from dog to dog.

HOME STAFFING

For the American Pit Bull Terrier owner who works during the day, a pet sitter or dog walker may be the perfect solution for the lonely pit bull longing for a midday stroll. Smart dog owners can approach local high schools or community centers if they don't know of a neighbor who is interested in a part-time commitment. Interview potential dog walkers and consider their experience with dogs, as well as your APBT's rapport with the candidate. (American Pit Bull Terriers are excellent judges of character.) Always check references before entrusting your dog and home to a new dog walker.

For an owner's long-term absence, such as a business trip or vacation, many American Pit Bull Terrier owners welcome the services of a pet sitter. It's usually less stressful on the dog to stay home with a pet sitter than to be boarded in a kennel. Pet sitters also may be more affordable than a week's stay at a full-service doggie day care.

Pet sitters must be even more reliable than dog walkers because the dog is depending on his surrogate owner for all of his needs for an extended period. Owners are advised to hire a certified pet sitter through the National Association of

Professional Pet Sitters, which can be accessed online at www.petsitters.org. NAPPS provides online and toll-free pet sitter locator services. The nonprofit organization certifies serious-minded, professional individuals who are knowledgeable in canine behavior, nutrition, health and safety. Always keep your American Pit Bull Terrier's best interest at heart when planning a trip.

SCHOOL'S IN SESSION

Puppy kindergarten, which is usually open to dogs between 3 to 6 months of age, allows puppies to learn and socialize with other dogs and people in a structured setting. Classes help your American Pit Bull Terrier enjoy going places with you and help your dog become a well-behaved member at public gatherings that include other dogs. They prepare him for adult obedience classes, as well as for life.

The problem with most puppy kindergarten classes is that they only occur one night a week. What about during the rest of the week?

If you're at home all week, you may be able to find other places to take your puppy, but you have to be careful about dog parks and other places where just any dog can go. An experience with a bully can undo all the good your classes have done, or worse, end in tragedy.

If you work, your puppy may be home alone all day, a tough situation for an American Pit Bull Terrier. Chances are he can't hold his urine in for that long, so your potty training will be undermined unless you're just aiming to teach him to use an indoor potty. And chances are, by the time you come home, he'll be bursting with energy, and you may start to think that he's hyperactive.

The answer for the professional with an American Pit Bull Terrier is doggie day care. Most larger cities have some sort of day care, whether it's a boarding kennel that keeps your dog in a run or a full-service day care that offers training, play time and even spa facilities. They range from a person who keeps a few dogs at his home to a state-of-the-art facility built just for dogs. Many of the more sophisticated doggie day cares offer webcams so you can see your dog throughout the day. Things to look for:

- escape-proof facilities, including a buffer between the dogs and any doors
- inoculation requirements for new dogs
- midday meals for young dogs
- obedience training (if offered), using reward-based methods
- safe and comfortable areas for sleeping
- screening of dogs for aggression
- small groups of similar sizes and ages
- toys and playground equipment, such as tunnels
- trained staff, with an adequate number to supervise the dogs (no more than 10 to 15 dogs per person)
- a webcam

Remember to keep your dog's leash slack when interacting with other dogs. It is not unusual for a dog to pick out one or two canine neighbors to dislike. If you know there's bad blood, step off to the side and put a barrier, such as a parked car, between the dogs. If there are no barriers to be had, move to the side of the walkway, cue your dog to sit, stay and watch you until his nemesis passes; then continue your walk.

SMART TIP!

CAR TRAVEL

You should accustom your American Pit Bull Terrier to riding in a car at an early age. You may or may not take him in the car often, but at the very least he will need to go to the vet, and you do not want these trips to be traumatic for the dog or troublesome for you. The safest way for a dog to ride in the car is in his crate. If he uses a crate in the house, you can use the same crate for travel.

Another option is a specially made safety harness for dogs, which straps your pit bull in the car much like a seat belt. Do not let the dog roam loose in the vehicle: This is very dangerous! If you should stop short, your dog can be thrown and injured. If the dog starts climbing on you and pes-

A smart owner will introduce his APBT to riding in the car at an early age to create a positive association.

tering you while you are driving, you will not be able to concentrate on the road. It is an unsafe situation for everyone — human and canine alike.

For long trips, stop often to let your APBT relieve himself. Take along whatever you need to clean up after him, including some paper towels for use should he have an accident in the car or suffer from motion sickness.

IDENTIFICATION

Your American Pit Bull Terrier is your valued companion and friend. That is why you always keep a close eye on him and you have made sure that he cannot escape from the yard or wriggle out of his collar and run away from you. However, accidents can happen and there may come a time when your dog unexpectedly gets separated from you. If this should occur, the first thing on your mind will be finding him. Proper identification, including an ID tag, a tattoo and possibly a microchip will increase the chances of him being returned to you safely and quickly.

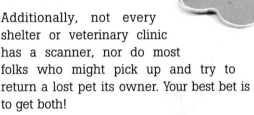

An ID tag on a collar or harness is the primary means of pet identification (ID licenses are required in many communities, anyway). Although inexpensive and easy to read, collars and ID tags can come off or be removed.

A microchip doesn't get lost. Containing a unique ID number that can be read by scanners, the microchip is embedded underneath a dog's skin. It's invaluable for identifying lost or stolen pets. However, to be effective, the microchip must be registered in a national database, and smart owners will be sure their contact info is kept up-to-date.

Additionally, not every shelter or veterinary clinic has a scanner, nor do most folks who might pick up and try to return a lost pet its owner. Your best bet is to get both!

Did You Know?

Some communities have created regular dog runs and separate spaces for small dogs. These dog runs are ideal for introducing puppies to the dog park experience. The runs and participants are smaller and their owners are often more vigilant because they are used to watching out for their fragile companions.

INDEX

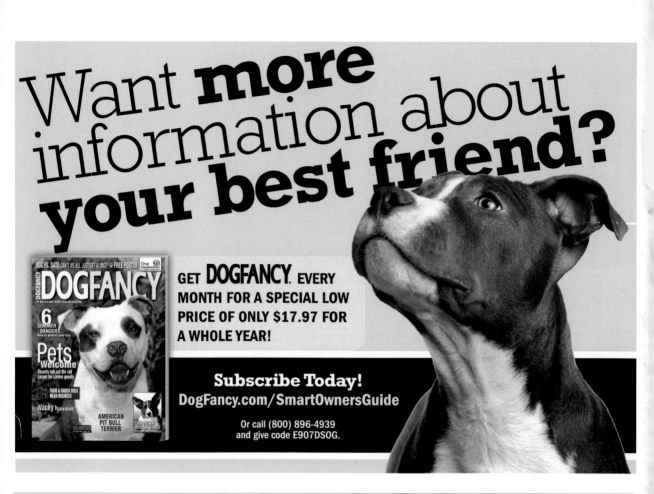

Want **more** information about your best friend?

GET **DOGFANCY.** EVERY MONTH FOR A SPECIAL LOW PRICE OF ONLY $17.97 FOR A WHOLE YEAR!

Subscribe Today!
DogFancy.com/SmartOwnersGuide

Or call (800) 896-4939
and give code E907DSOG.

AMERICAN PIT BULL TERRIER, a Smart Owner's Guide®

part of the Kennel Club Books® Interactive Series®

LIBRARY OF CONGRESS CATALOGING-IN-PUBLICATION DATA
   American pit bull terrier / from the editors of Dog fancy magazine.
      p. cm. -- (Smart owner's guide)
   Includes bibliographical references and index.
   ISBN 978-1-59378-759-2
   1. American pit bull terrier. I. Dog fancy (San Juan Capistrano, Calif.)
   SF429.A72A487 2010
   636.755'9--dc22

                              2009029700

JOIN **Club APBT®** TODAY!